A

PROSECUTION OF
THE MENTALLY
DISTURBED

PROSECUTION OF THE MENTALLY DISTURBED

DILEMMAS OF IDENTIFICATION AND DISCRETION

D CHISWICK
M W McISAAC
F H McCLINTOCK

ABERDEEN UNIVERSITY PRESS

First published 1984
Aberdeen University Press
A member of the Pergamon Group

British Library Cataloguing in Publication Data

Chiswick, D
   Prosecution of the mentally disturbed
   1.   Insanity—Jurisprudence—Great Britain
   2.   Prosecution—Great Britain
   I.   Title   II. McIsaac, M W
   III. McClintock, F H
   344.105'5042'0880824   KD 7897

   ISBN 0-08-028481-7

PRINTED IN GREAT BRITAIN
THE UNIVERSITY PRESS
ABERDEEN

Foreword

Mentally abnormal offenders must be regarded as persons *sui generis*. They must not be confused with either ordinary criminals or ordinary mental patients. They deserve our sympathy because they are mentally afflicted, but they must be kept in conditions of adequate security, if they have displayed indications of dangerousness.

Sympathetic treatment and maintenance of security do not combine easily. This has always caused a problem for the sentencer, but the problem is not confined to that stage in the proceedings. Those with responsibility in the earlier stages—in Scotland: the police, the prosecutor, the psychiatrist and the sheriff—all have problems in relation to the management of persons who have committed acts which would be crimes, if committed by a mentally normal person, but who may be suffering from some mental abnormality. How is any abnormality identified? Where should the person be kept for observation? Who can best observe? These are only some of the questions which require an answer in relation to the time of arrest. Obviously if the accused is not identified as being mentally abnormal, he will not receive the benefit of any system set up to deal with such persons, and therefore, although it may be very difficult, an attempt must be made to distinguish such persons from the ordinary criminals.

We are greatly indebted to Derek Chiswick, Mary McIsaac and Derick McClintock for this book which sets out most clearly the problems associated with the mentally abnormal offender at the various stages of proceedings after arrest. It does not pretend to offer perfect solutions to all the problems, but careful study does show pointers in certain directions. I sincerely hope that those responsible for criminal and mental health legislation and administration will find guidance and inspiration from this book to improve the lot of that unfortunate member of our society, the mentally abnormal offender.

W G Chalmers
Crown Agent
March 1984

Contents

Table of Statutes

Acknowledgements

We are very grateful to all those within the criminal justice and medical systems in Scotland who, by permitting access to their records, by providing information, and by discussing matters freely with us made this research project possible. We must specially thank Mr W G Chalmers, the Crown Agent, whose initial support made finance available through Treasury funding. We have had the great advantage of his advice and support throughout the research study in Scotland. The empirical study was undertaken during a two-year period by one of us, Mrs Mary W McIsaac, who was assisted in the analysis of materials by Miss I Gawler. Our thanks are due to Miss Lydia Lawson for typing the report and assisting in its preparation for publication.

Chapter 1

Introduction

The Criminal Justice and the Medical processes of social control

The relationship between criminal justice and the identification and control, or treatment, of the mentally abnormal offender continues to be a subject fraught with theoretical difficulties and practical complexities. The extensive writings on this subject by philosophers, jurists, psychiatrists and criminologists provide ample evidence of the problems which perplex the various professions involved in these matters; while the regular appearance of news items and articles in the Press, together with radio and television coverage, gives some indication of the extent of general public concern—if not indeed at times anxiety—over a number of issues relating to mentally abnormal offenders.

What one is confronted with in relation to the mentally abnormal offender is the interface between two different perspectives and control processes: the legal and the medical. The former, which is primarily within the domain of the criminal law, is concerned with the establishment of guilt, or responsibility, for the unlawful behaviour, thus leading to the right for the agents of the State on behalf of society to impose punishment; while the latter is concerned with the extent to which mental abnormality leads to the impairment or the diminishing of individual responsibility and the need to have primary regard to the welfare of the individual concerned through psychiatric or other forms of treatment in order to attempt a cure. Clearly, the criminal justice and the medical processes can, both theoretically and with respect to particular cases, be in conflict with each other.

The general contrast between the two control processes has been heightened in recent years as a result of the steady decline in the acceptance of the ideas of reformation or rehabilitation of offenders through penal processes. This was a reversal of an earlier trend based upon the emergence of the ideology of paternalistic state welfare which was dominant through until the 1970s. The earlier period of 'penological optimism', which was fairly general in Western European countries, could be characterised on the one hand by both the content of the criminal law and the processes of criminal justice being regarded as unproblematic, with the latter being based on the concept of legality rather than that of expediency, and on the other hand by the control of crime being seen as the full development of penal reformation in the treatment of offenders, i.e. the philosophy of 'penal treatment'. During that earlier period there was a general consensus as to aims between those responsible for crime control, the administrators

FIGURE 1
Social control

	I *Penal* *criminal justice*	II *Therapeutic* *(+ social work)*	III *Educational* *(+ social work)*	IV *Compensatory* *(civil or* *criminal law)*	V *Conciliatory* *(civil, criminal* *or social)*
(1) *Standard*	Prohibition	Normality	Educated	Obligation	Harmony
(2) *Problem*	Guilty	Need	Ignorance/incompetence	Debt	Conflict
(3) *Initiation of action*	(i) agency of community (police) (ii) victim	(i) agency of community (ii) deviant	(i) agency of community (ii) student	(i) agency of community (ii) victim	(i) agency of group (ii) disputants
(4) *Identity of deviant/or 'problem' individual*	Offender	Patient/client	Ignorant, uneducated or incompetent person	Debtor	Disputant
(5) *Solution/or goal*	Punishment	Help	Standard, certification or recognition of competence	Payment (in cash or kind)	Resolution of conflict

Source: Adapted from Black, *Behaviour of Law* (1976) and modified by F H McClintock

of the criminal justice system, the psychiatric services to the courts and researchers into criminological and penological issues. In fact, forensic psychiatry was seen at that stage as in the vanguard of reformation of offenders and its treatment model was applied in the non-medical penal processes. If one applies the modified social control models, originally developed by Donald Black[1] (see Figure 1), it can be seen that during the twentieth century the Penal or Criminal Justice Model (I) incorporated within its structure the Therapeutic (II), the Educational (III), the Compensatory (IV) and the Conciliatory (V) models. This 'muddling of the models' extended the scope of criminal justice and legitimised the use of the professional helping-services in the control of crime.[2] The role of the psychiatrist became crucial in the emergence of that process.

As is well known, in recent years all this has changed so that the earlier optimism has given way to penological agnosticism as regards the impact of the criminal justice processes on the prevention of crime and of recidivism. A noticeable decline in the acceptance of rehabilitation as the primary goal in criminal justice is viewed by some as a sign of growing cynicism, others describe it as a penological crisis; but among the public at large, among academic scholars, policy-makers and practitioners, there is a growing awareness of an incipient dissatisfaction with the administration of criminal justice in general, as well as severally with each major segment, such as policing practices, prosecution, trial and sentencing, and the impact of penal measures.

Very substantial shifts in attitudes have also lately affected medical and psychiatric developments, especially in the sphere of forensic studies: thus, the expansionist approach to the positive role of the psychiatrist which dominated doctrine in the early part of the century has been replaced by a substantial reduction of their claims and a curtailment of their involvement with respect to the control and treatment of offenders, thus sharpening the differences between the medical and penal perspectives. This is not the appropriate occasion on which to review the complex processes leading to the fundamental changes that have shaped the contemporary attitudes of the so-called 'post-rehabilitative era'.[3] However, they cannot be ignored when practical problems are judged, specific policy changes are contemplated, and applied research is undertaken.

The aims of the research

The present study has developed from a research project into considerations of mental abnormality at the arrest and prosecution stages in Scotland. Subsequently, it was extended to consider a number of more general issues relating to mental abnormality and crime, with special comparative references to the situation as prevailing in England and Wales.

The two primary aims of the Scottish project were: (1) to discover the specific measures available for ascertaining whether an alleged offender is suffering from a mental disorder which necessitates special treatment or

1 References start on p 122

handling in the course of bringing him to justice or diverting him solely to medical treatment and supervision; and (2) to give the background information for considering the possibilities of improvement, in both legal and medical arrangements and services. In that regard therefore the study should be seen as one of applied criminology, or what Professor J Hall has aptly described as research into 'law as action'.[4]

As already indicated, the specific research field is thus located at the interface between the criminal justice control system, with its emphasis on due process, establishment of guilt and the punishment of offenders; and the medical control system, with its emphasis on the diagnosis of disorders of patients in need of alleviation or cure. In a wider context a number of issues are raised especially those relating to discretionary powers, that have to be regarded in the light of the nature and purposes of the criminal justice processes, the rights of the individual, as against those of the officials of the State, in relation to the use of medical facilities, and the various forms of accountability governing the actions of the agents employed by the State in the criminal justice process. These more general issues are, of course, important to all countries governed by parliamentary democracies.

The criminal justice system is organised to process the normal offender through the various stages of arrest, prosecution, conviction and sentence. As will be shown, issues relating to mental health arise only in relation to a small proportion of those going through the criminal justice process, while the majority of those who come within the care of the psychiatric services have never been in contact with the criminal justice process. This research study focuses on the prosecution process and hence on the role of the procurators fiscal in the context of policing and the provision of medical services for the mentally disturbed. The study in Scotland was designed to provide information on several specific questions:

1 What action do the police take when they suspect that an arrested person may be mentally unwell?
2 Are mental-health doctors prepared to attend at the cells for examination of such persons?
3 Are facilities available to take such persons to hospital immediately?
4 Is the procurator fiscal consulted about such cases?
5 Do police report their suspicions, and any action taken, to the fiscal in cases where the accused is kept in custody?
6 If they do, what action does the procurator fiscal then take?
7 Are the courts prepared to send accused to hospital on remand, rather than to prison, and are there adequate hospital facilities for such remands?

In the initial stages it was necessary firstly to carry out research in order to identify the size of the problems as known to the police, the prosecutors and the courts, and secondly, how the agencies involved operated in the various regions of Scotland, the reasons for their mode of operation and the consequences of their choice. Such empirical data provided the context in which to examine decision-making and the exercise of discretion and thus led on to a consideration of the wider issues of social control and individual rights of citizens.

The Scottish research study has been based upon two sources of information:

1 from official case documentation contained in police records, prosecutors' files, court records and prison records of medical officers; and

2 structured interviews with representatives of all police forces, some members of all procurator fiscal regions, a selection of sheriffs, psychiatrists in a range of mental hospitals, some social workers and some prison staff members.

The factual data covered (a) the precipitating incident, (b) basic social data regarding the alleged offender, (c) reasons for requesting medical or psychiatric advice, (d) the source of advice and the advice given, and (e) the outcome of the case. This was then related to the opinions and the views obtained from interviews, and thus it was possible to place in a contextual framework the use of discretion and the practice of decision-making on the part of those operating the services involved in dealing with offenders who were possibly mentally abnormal. (Details of the sampling frame and some basic data relating thereto are provided in Appendix II below, p 110.)

In the preparation of this monograph from the Scottish research report it was also possible to utilise relevant information on equivalent aspects of the processes from the system in England and Wales, together with the knowledge and experience of two of the authors who at an earlier stage had been directly involved in research and practice relating to the criminal justice processes and the medical services in the English system. The present study provides, first of all, the medico-legal framework within which practical issues relating to the mentally abnormal offender have to be dealt with. This is then followed by chapters which consider successively the procedures and problems facing the police, the prosecutors, the courts and the medical services. The final chapter provides some specific recommendations based upon the Scottish research project and some general conclusions in a wider context.

Chapter 2

The Medico-Legal Framework

Each year in Scotland well over half a million crimes or offences are made known to the police and approximately a quarter of a million people have criminal proceedings taken against them in court. Widely differing explanations for this bulk of criminal activity would be advanced by social scientists, politicians, jurists and academics, some of whom would argue that any person whose behaviour brings him into conflict with the law has problems in adjusting to society's requirements and that these problems stem from psychological difficulties within the individual. Such a view denotes a highly simplistic approach to the complexities of criminal behaviour, and a societal perspective or perhaps a multifactorial approach drawing on cultural factors, individual psychology, law-enforcement practices and penal policy is more likely to be generally acceptable. However great or small is the contribution of an individual's personality or psychological make-up to his criminal behaviour, the fact is that the great majority of offenders pass through the criminal justice system without any reference being made to their mental state. Most cases are processed without invoking any medical opinion or judgement, on the basis that there is an initial assumption of the accused person being sane in mind and responsible for his actions. However, for a tiny minority of accused persons a medical opinion is sought at any of a number of stages in arrest and prosecution.

When doctors are invited to play a part in the criminal justice process they are being asked to operate in a system whose primary function is the detection and prosecution of crime. This is clearly different from their more familiar environment where the chief function is the provision of health care. The distinction is more than merely theoretical, for the doctor performing a forensic task must observe the ground rules of the system which he enters, and his recommendations must be realistic in the context in which his opinion is invited. Discussion in this chapter is principally concerned with the working practices and legal regulations within which the doctor advising upon mentally abnormal offenders is required to function. Where the legal and medical professions inter-act there are always problems of definition. Unfortunately the same words are used by different professional groups with quite different meanings. Not only may the legal use of a particular term be different from its medical use but it may also differ widely from the layman's understanding of the same expression. If terms such as 'mental abnormality', 'mental illness' and 'mental disorder' are regarded as virtually synonymous with each other, much confusion will arise in any ensuing discussion. The expressions convey different meanings to legal, medical and lay people and therefore some attempt at definition is a necessary preliminary to any discussion.

6

Mental abnormality

'Mental abnormality' is a very broad term which may be applied to all those forms of mental functioning which can be said to differ from the statistical norm. The designation of an individual as mentally abnormal merely signifies that one or perhaps many aspects of his mental functioning differ from those of most people. It does not signify that a mental illness or disease accounts for the mental abnormality, even although in certain cases this might very well be so. The term 'mentally abnormal' applied to a person simply indicates that he is different without specifying the nature or the cause of the difference. The Butler Report gave as examples of this category religious fanatics, occasional drunks and even people with unusual mental capacities such as photographic memories. Thus the fact that someone is a religious fanatic does not mean he suffers from a mental illness but it does mean he differs in his mental functioning from most members of society.

Insanity

The term 'insanity' is something of a legal relic which has ceased to convey any clear psychiatric meaning. However, it continues to have legal usage and probably is an attractive term for lawyers to employ because it carries the implication of a total lack of responsibility for any criminal act. It is an 'all-or-nothing' term which is out of phase with current psychiatric thought because it is now recognised that psychiatric conditions, or indeed illnesses, are not the sole determinants of the sufferer's behaviour. A person's criminal behaviour may be influenced, but not totally controlled, by a psychiatric illness and in some cases criminal behaviour may be totally unrelated to an underlying mental condition. Moreover the use of the term 'insanity' implies a state of permanence whereas in fact the severity of a mental illness can vary in any individual with time. It is quite possible to be legally insane at one moment but legally sane a few weeks (or even days) later.

The term is not used in current psychiatric practice and indeed it does not appear in the Mental Health Acts of 1959 and 1983. It is only used in the Scottish Mental Health Act 1960 in Section 63 which refers to the procedure to be followed where verdicts of 'insanity in bar of trial' or 'acquittal on the ground of insanity' are returned. Although an obsolete term in psychiatry it presumably refers to a severe form of mental illness where there is a gross disturbance of thought, feeling and perception.

Mental disorder

'Mental disorder', on the other hand, is a term which does appear in both the English and Scottish Mental Health Acts and it carries the implication that the condition in question should, if possible, be treated. The spectrum of mental disorders ranges from those which may be readily treatable by the family doctor to those which warrant compulsory treatment in hospital. In addition there are mental disorders for which there is no known satisfactory treatment. Thus mental disorders vary both in their severity and their susceptibility to treatment. Moreover the severity and nature of a mental disorder in an individual can alter from time to time so that there may be periods of quiescence and periods of disturbance. Whilst most forms of mental disorder are not permanent in nature, many have a tendency to recur. This periodicity of certain conditions means that the relevance of that disorder for legal purposes can change in the same individual on different occasions.

Mental illness

'Mental illness' for legal purposes is one of the sub-categories of mental disorder. In the Mental Health Act 1983 there are three other sub-categories, namely psychopathic disorder, mental impairment and severe mental impairment. In Scotland only the two categories, mental illness and mental deficiency, are recognised in the 1960 Act, but the differences between England and Scotland in this respect are more apparent than real. The category 'mental illness' in Scotland is further sub-divided to include 'a mental illness which is a persistent disorder manifested only by abnormally aggressive or seriously irresponsible conduct'. This rather unwieldy phrase is almost exactly the same as the English Mental Health Act definition of psychopathic disorder. Thus for practical purposes the fact that there are four sub-categories of mental disorder in England and only two in Scotland is of little importance. For psychiatrists the term mental illness denotes a mental condition which is distinct both from a disorder of personality and from mental handicap. Like the term 'mental disorder' it covers a range of illnesses from self-limiting conditions, such as an anxiety neurosis, to severely disabling diseases such as schizophrenia or senile dementia. In view of the broad range of conditions to which the generic term 'mental illness' is applied, it is not surprising that neither the English nor Scottish Acts offer any definition of the term.

The identification of mental disorder

The psychiatric conclusion that a person convicted of a bizarre crime does not suffer from a mental illness at first sight appears puzzling to the non-psychiatrist. Indeed such a finding often provokes such a wry comment as 'that means the person who killed this child is normal'. This illustrates a problem which is only partly one of semantics. Clearly anyone who kills a child is not normal, because most people do not kill children, and the behaviour is therefore a deviation from the norm. However, because the assailant is abnormal in the statistical sense it does not necessarily follow that he is abnormal in the psychiatric sense, although he might be. Furthermore even though he might be mentally abnormal it does not follow that his mental abnormality constitutes a mental illness. It might constitute a disorder of personality, or possibly the assailant might have been rendered mentally abnormal in his functioning as a result of alcohol intoxication. In both these examples being personality-disordered or inebriated might render the person mentally abnormal in his behaviour but not mentally ill.

The problem is more than just a problem of semantics however and partly stems from the manner in which the public assume mental illness is diagnosed or detected. There is a temptation to regard all abnormal behaviour as the consequence of mental disorder. Such a view gave rise to the now obsolete practice of identifying 'illnesses' such as kleptomania, dypsomania and pyromania. This fashion for classifying what were referred to as 'the monomanias' has long since passed. It is, however, true that abnormal behaviour is in itself a common precipitant for psychiatric referral, but in arriving at a diagnosis the psychiatrist considers much more than the behaviour alone. The behaviour and the circumstances in which it occurred are important considerations in establishing the diagnosis, but it is equally important to have details of the individual's personal history, medical history and family history. In this way a global rather than a 'snapshot' assessment can be made of the presenting behaviour. Finally the psychiatrist evaluates the features he finds in his face-to-face examination of the patient and on occasions certain investigations (e.g. a blood test or an electro-encephalogram) might be required to complete the assessment. Thus it is not possible to conclude on the basis of behaviour alone whether or not an individual is mentally disordered.

Abnormal behaviour can alert various agencies to the possibility that mental disorder exists, but by itself it does not provide confirmatory evidence of any such disorder. A man who shouts in the street and threatens passers-by with a knife may be eccentric, drunk, politically motivated, mentally disordered, or simply angry and this list is by no means exhaustive. A description of his behaviour alone says nothing of the underlying cause. Describing everybody who behaves in a peculiar manner as 'mad' might be an understandable social response to certain forms of odd behaviour but it is a grossly misleading over-simplification; it so broadens the meaning of the term 'mad' that it becomes virtually useless.

Pathways of psychiatric referral

The psychiatrist may be involved in the assessment and treatment of offender patients at a number of different stages in the arrest and prosecution process. His advice might be sought at the time of apprehension

by the police, during police custody but before appearing in court, during
the period of remand before the trial, after conviction but before sentence
and finally during a period of imprisonment. The terms of reference for the
psychiatrist at each of these different stages are slightly different and they
depend upon the particular requirements of the law-enforcement or judicial
agency which seeks the medical advice. The analysis of the medical intervention at three of these stages (arrest, prosecution and sentence) is considered
in detail in subsequent chapters. The psychiatric conclusion given to the
referring agency is of functional importance and may be a major
determinant of outcome for the offender. Thus the opinion is more than a
medical statement of fact; it can crucially affect the next stage in the arrest
and prosecution process.

The referral of an individual for psychiatric examination by the police or
the courts differs from the conventional psychiatric referral in another very
important area, namely that which concerns the person's willingness, or
otherwise, to be examined. Most patients are referred to psychiatrists by
their family doctors and the very fact that they keep their appointment at
the psychiatric clinic suggests that they wish to be seen and are willingly
seeking medical attention. Forensic referrals, however, are initiated, not by
the patient seeking help, but by others deciding that it is an appropriate
step. Admittedly some forensic patients might be perfectly happy to see a
psychiatrist, but equally some may not and a reluctant meeting with a
psychiatrist can be coloured by an unco-operative or hostile attitude. The
psychiatrist, too, has altered terms of reference in dealing with the forensic
referral. He is accustomed to considering the best interests of the patient as
his principal concern, but some might say that in the forensic case his first
obligation is to the agency seeking his opinion. In practice, as the following
chapters describe, few cases can be neatly considered in such black and
white terms and most decisions are probably based on an overall view of
what is best for the patient *and* for the referring agency.

Legislation and the mentally abnormal offender

Complex legislation governs the procedures for dealing with mentally
abnormal offenders and certain aspects of the law differ widely north and
south of the Border. This description of some of the legislation is not
intended to be exhaustive and detail is included in the Appendix.

If the police apprehend an individual whom they believe to be mentally
disordered they have two methods available for obtaining a medical opinion.
They can take the subject to a hospital for examination or they can summon
a doctor to attend at the police station. The Mental Health Acts (section 136
in England and section 104 in Scotland) enable a policeman to remove a
person believed to be mentally disordered from a public place to a place of
safety for the purpose of psychiatric examination. The function of the
examination is to enable the doctor at the hospital to make 'any necessary

arrangement' for the treatment or care of the individual. For this purpose the person may be detained in the hospital for up to seventy-two hours, although the law does not direct that he must be detained for this length of time.

When a doctor examines a person at the police station his remit depends largely on whether or not that person has been charged with any offence. If no charge has been made (and none is likely) then the options available to the doctor are similar to those in any psychiatric consultation; the only difference is in the location of the examination. The doctor might conclude that no treatment is indicated or he might suggest admission to a psychiatric hospital. Depending on circumstances that admission could take place either on an informal basis (i.e. with the patient's agreement) or it could be on a compulsory basis under Part IV of the Mental Health (Scotland) Act 1960, which is concerned with civil commitment to hospital.

The circumstances are altered if the doctor is examining an individual who has already been charged with an offence by the police and is being held in custody. The doctor's remit strictly speaking is limited to a consideration of the accused person's mental fitness or otherwise to remain in police custody. In practice this question often becomes blurred into the more general one of the appropriateness for that person of immediate hospitalisation as opposed to confinement in a police cell. The legal options available to the doctor range from making no medical recommendation at all to recommending immediate admission to a psychiatric hospital. If he does suggest immediate hospitalisation, whether on an informal basis or under the Mental Health Acts, then it only takes place with the agreement of the police authority. Between these options of 'no recommendation' and 'immediate admission' a third option is available to the doctor, who can either recommend verbally to the police or in writing, that certain psychiatric factors should be brought to the attention of the court when the case is first considered by them. It would then be open to the court to obtain medical reports on the accused person before proceeding further. Such reports are usually obtained by remanding the individual either in prison or on bail and then instructing a doctor to examine him.

In Scotland authority exists under sections 25 and 330 of the Criminal Procedure (Scotland) Act 1975 to remand an accused to a hospital for further examination. This can only be effected if prior to the court appearance the accused person has been examined by a doctor who recommends a remand to hospital. It has many advantages which are further discussed in Chapter 8, and a similar measure has recently been introduced in England in section 35 of the Mental Health Act 1983.

Many defendants are referred for psychiatric examination during the period prior to their trial. Such an assessment may take place upon a defendant who is in custody or in the community and it can be initiated either by the prosecution or the defence. At this stage the remit of the psychiatrist covers three basic areas. Firstly he is required to give an opinion on the defendant's fitness to plead. The second task is to make some comment on the defendant's responsibility for his actions, although in

Scotland this is virtually confined to cases of indictable crimes which are being prosecuted on solemn procedure. Finally the psychiatrist is expected to indicate whether or not he feels a psychiatric disposal would be appropriate in the event of conviction. When a psychiatric report is requested after conviction but before sentence, then the first two tasks described above are 'dead' issues and the only function of the report is in relation to disposal or sentence.

Fitness to plead

It is an important principle of law that it would be unjust to try a person who by reason of mental disorder is unable to defend himself. Thus before a plea can be taken from a defendant in court he must be 'fit to plead'. This is in fact a colloquial and not a legal expression; the relevant legislation is contained in section 4 of the Criminal Procedure (Insanity) Act 1964 and the Mental Health (Scotland) Act 1960 in section 63. In England the criteria for fitness to plead depend on the accused person being able to:

1 understand the nature of the charge against him;
2 distinguish between a plea of guilty and not guilty;
3 give instructions to his lawyer;
4 follow the evidence in court;
5 challenge a juror to whom he might object.

In Scotland the criterion for fitness to plead has been more broadly interpreted and simply depends on the defendant's ability to instruct his lawyer in the same way as a sane man would do. Furthermore, section 63 of the Scottish Mental Health Act links the fitness to plead issue with the legal but undefined concept of insanity, so that a finding of insanity almost automatically implies unfitness to plead. The result of the different interpretation and wording of the law in Scotland is that findings of unfitness to plead are returned ten times more frequently in Scotland than in England. Indeed the verdict is quite rare in England but in Scotland it accounts for nearly half of those mental hospital admissions which are ordered by the court each year (Chiswick, 1978).[1]

The mandatory disposal of those persons found unfit to plead is committal to a mental hospital on a compulsory basis and in Scotland detention is in terms of Part V of the Mental Health (Scotland) Act 1960. An order restricting discharge (see below) is automatically added in England and may in some circumstances be made in Scotland. There is no time limit set for the period to be spent in hospital.

The laws relating to fitness to plead have been much criticised on two main grounds: firstly, the question of guilt or innocence is never established and, secondly, the mandatory hospital disposal which follows such a finding may effectively be detention for life. Both the Butler Report in England[2] and the Thomson Report in Scotland[3] made a number of

recommendations for changing the law. The basic aims of their recommendations were twofold. The first aim was to reduce to a minimum those
instances where no trial takes place and in those cases to provide some
means of examining the facts of the case. The second aim was to introduce
flexibility into the disposal option available to the court where a defendant
was too mentally ill to be tried.

Mental responsibility

If a defendant is mentally well enough to stand trial it remains possible for
him to be acquitted, and therefore exonerated of guilt, where evidence is
accepted that he was insane at the time of committing the crime. Any person
found to be insane at the time of his crime cannot be held legally responsible, and therefore guilty, for that behaviour. In such cases a verdict of
'not guilty by reason of insanity' is returned in England and one of
'acquittal on the grounds of insanity' is returned in Scotland. The plea is
usually referred to as the insanity defence, and although in theory it is
logical, in practice it is very rarely used. In England there have been only
one or two such cases each year in the last decade. The criteria of insanity
for this defence are contained in the time-honoured but obsolete
McNaughton Rules which were established in 1843. The wording of these
rules is so rigid that today few cases fall within their interpretation and this,
coupled with the requirement to prove the insanity 'beyond reasonable
doubt', has made the insanity plea unpopular with defence lawyers.

A further disadvantage of the verdict is that, like the unfit to plead
verdict, it results in mandatory committal to a hospital under the terms of a
hospital order with a restriction order without limit of time. Moreover the
hospital is usually a maximum security (special) hospital (see below). This
disposal has been criticised in the Butler and Thomson Reports on the
grounds that it might cause an individual who is not suffering from a mental
disorder at the time of his trial to be incarcerated in hospital indefinitely.
Some flexibility in the method of disposal of the acquitted person has been
suggested. In addition the Butler Committee proposed a novel psychiatric
test for the insanity defence to replace the out-dated McNaughton Rules.

In almost all crimes responsibility, in legal terms, is an all-or-nothing
affair. The defendant can either be responsible for his actions (and therefore guilty) or not responsible for them (and therefore not guilty). However,
for murder, and only for murder, a halfway stage of reduced or diminished
responsibility is recognised. It has been part of Scottish law since 1867 and
was introduced into England by the Homicide Act of 1957. The plea of
diminished responsibility rests upon evidence that shows the accused person
to have been suffering from an abnormality of mind which substantially
impaired his responsibility for the act of killing. A successful plea has the
effect of reducing a charge of murder to one of manslaughter in England
and culpable homicide in Scotland. The virtue of the plea and the reduction

in charge is that it introduces flexibility into the disposal option available to the court, in place of the mandatory life sentence that follows conviction for murder. A person convicted of manslaughter or culpable homicide, but not murder, could for example be ordered to hospital, or placed on probation, or even be given an absolute discharge.

Psychiatric advice concerning disposal

After trial and conviction the court is faced with the task of sentencing. This is the responsibility of the bench or judge but medical evidence may be heard where this seems appropriate. The psychiatric opinion is nothing more than just that, and the court is not obliged to accept the doctor's recommendations. The various alternatives which are available to the psychiatrist are as follows:

1 a recommendation for compulsory admission to hospital;
2 a recommendation for informal admission to hospital, perhaps as part of a probation order;
3 a recommendation for out-patient treatment, perhaps as part of a probation order;
4 no psychiatric recommendation.

Compulsory admission to hospital after criminal proceedings may be ordered by the court under the terms of a hospital order (section 37 of the Mental Health Act 1983 and sections 175 and 376 of the Criminal Procedure (Scotland) Act 1975). Such a disposal accounts for a tiny proportion (less than 1 in 2000) of those persons prosecuted each year. The principle of the hospital order is that the penal disposal is waived and admission to a psychiatric hospital for treatment is substituted. The many different factors which determine whether or not these orders are made are considered in detail in subsequent chapters. There are many legal regulations which govern the making of the orders but the most important of them are as follows. The crime must be one which is punishable by imprisonment; the crime must be one for which the penalty is not fixed by law, which excludes murder (mandatory life imprisonment sentence) but not manslaughter; the convicted person must be suffering from a mental disorder within the meaning of the Mental Health Acts. The court, having regard to all the circumstances, must feel it the most appropriate means of disposal; two doctors must support the recommendation and one of these must be an approved specialist in psychiatry. Once a patient is admitted to hospital under a hospital order, the total control of the patient rests with the consultant in charge who can discharge him whenever he feels it is appropriate. Thus it is theoretically possible, but practically unlikely, for a patient to be ordered into hospital by the court and be discharged by the doctor in charge twenty-four hours later.

About twenty per cent of hospital orders made annually carry an additional restriction order which can be imposed by the court when it feels there is a question of public safety involved. This removes total control of the patient from the responsible medical officer and places it in the hands of the Home Secretary in England or the Secretary of State in Scotland who must give approval before the patient can be transferred to another hospital, discharged, or sent on leave of absence. Restriction orders are most commonly imposed without limit of time and can thus effectively mean detention for life. The manner in which the Home Secretary or Secretary of State reaches a decision in any individual case is not made public and until recently the patient had no right of appeal to a judicial body with executive powers. Following the conclusion of the European Court of Human Rights that such detention was a breach of Article 5(4) of the European Convention on Human Rights, legislative change in the United Kingdom has been introduced (Department of Health and Social Security et al. 1981)[4] in section 70 of the Mental Health Act 1983.

In some instances the examining psychiatrist may conclude that the convicted person suffers from a mental disorder, but that it is not of a nature that warrants compulsory admission to hospital in terms of the Mental Health Acts. In these circumstances it is possible for him to recommend informal treatment as a condition of a probation order under the powers of the Criminal Courts Act 1973 or the Criminal Procedure (Scotland) Act 1975. The treatment may be as an in-patient or as an out-patient but it specifically excludes admission to a maximum security (special) hospital. The psychiatric probation order is potentially of considerable value, providing an opportunity to treat an individual whose psychiatric problem falls short of the legal concept of mental disorder. Should the patient fail to comply with the treatment (e.g. fail to keep out-patient clinic appointments) then the probation officer has the authority to return the offender to court as having been in breach of probation.

Treatment can be made available to an offender on an informal basis without any legal conditions operating. The court may be happy to accept the fact that treatment is offered and the person simply agrees to attend. In Scotland this informal treatment is sometimes combined with a deferred sentence. Here the court defers sentence for, say, six months during which time it expects the offender to undergo psychiatric treatment which has been offered. When the case is reconsidered six months later the court can take into account any response to treatment before finally disposing of the case.

If the psychiatrist reporting to the court does not feel that any treatment whatsoever is indicated then he makes no recommendation and in these circumstances it is impossible for the court to make any form of medical treatment disposal. Occasionally the bench, in passing sentence of imprisonment, recommends that a prisoner receives psychiatric treatment whilst in prison. There can be no guarantee that a recommendation of this type will be acted upon because the type of prison to which an offender is sent, and the availability of psychiatric treatment within it, are matters upon which the court has no jurisdiction.

The Mental Health Acts of Scotland and England both contain regula-

tions in respect of special hospitals for those patients who 'require treatment under conditions of special security on account of their dangerous,
violent or criminal propensities'. Whilst all the patients within the special
hospitals are compulsorily detained under the Mental Health Acts, they are
not all offenders. Approximately twenty-five per cent of the patients have
been transferred from ordinary hospitals for the mentally ill or mentally
handicapped, having originally been admitted to them under civil
procedures. Broadmoor, Rampton, Moss-side and Park Lane Hospitals are
in England and the State Hospital at Carstairs serves Scotland. Admissions
to the special hospitals are controlled differently in England and Scotland.
In England admissions are determined by the Department of Health and
Social Security, acting as managers of the English special hospitals. If a
court recommends a special hospital disposal the application is considered
by the Department of Health and Social Security but there is no obligation
to provide a bed. In Scotland, where a court makes a hospital order, it is
required to specify to which hospital it is sending the patient. Moreover it
can only make such a recommendation when it has received evidence that a
bed is indeed available at that hospital (sections 175 and 376 of the Criminal
Procedure (Scotland) Act 1975) within twenty-eight days of making the
order. Thus the matter is determined by prior consultation between the
doctors recommending the hospital order and the Physician Superintendent
of the State Hospital, or equally so of any other hospital where hospital
order admission is recommended.

Chapter 3

The Police

Nigel Walker has referred to the 'long-drawn conflict between justice and
expediency' and it is suggested that the decisions that have to be made by
the varying groups dealing with the mentally abnormal in the criminal
justice process can be examined in these two terms, expediency and justice.
It is also suggested that decisions can be seen as lay or professional. As far
as detecting mental abnormality is concerned, the police officer is a layman
deciding on the appropriate steps to be taken with an alleged offender
subject to the expediency of the immediate circumstances. It is one of a
series of decisions, each of which may be based on differing criteria, made
under pressure in a busy police station. But the police officer is also a
citizen, a member of the community, responsive to the needs of that
community and responsible for his own actions in seeking to serve it. Thus a
heavy burden of personal responsibility is laid on the police officer who
finds himself faced with the need to decide at the beginning of the criminal
justice process whether or not an alleged offender may be mentally
disordered.

Para. 17 of the Police (Scotland) Act 1967 states: '. . . it shall be the duty
of the constables of a police force . . . where an offence has been
committed . . . to make such reports to the appropriate prosecutor, as may
be necessary for the purpose of bringing the offender with all due speed to
justice . . . to take every precaution to ensure that any person charged with
an offence *is not unreasonably and unnecessarily detained* in custody
. . . the chief constable shall comply with such lawful instructions as he
may receive from the appropriate prosecutor' [our italics]. The immediate
decision therefore relates to detention in custody, and the lay police officer
may seek professional medical, or more specifically psychiatric, advice.
Clearly this cannot be sought for every detainee; interest must therefore
focus on when it is sought, how it is sought, and whether it is sought in the
appropriate cases.

When the issue of police training for handling or recognising mental
abnormality was discussed with senior police officers in Scotland, the
general opinion was that this was a matter of learning through experience.
As in so many aspects of police work, young officers learn the feel of the
situation through working with more experienced men. Apart from understandable and immediate rejection of any suggestion of yet more subjects
being added to formal training, there was a considered view that the
police do not want, and should not be made, to become 'mini-
psychiatrists'. The only officer who argued cogently for the opposite view
was one who himself had been for many years involved in voluntary work
with the mentally ill in hospital and in the community, and who felt that

the knowledge and experience he had gained was of great value to him in his police work.

In general the feeling was that police were better 'knowing nothing' in a professional sense: that they were laymen in touch with the public, themselves members of that public, and that in their decision-making they were reflecting public attitudes to mental disorder.[1] Any formal training could upset this balance, but also the lack of such training may be seen as professional protection for an individual officer, should an error of judgement be alleged.

Within the framework of reporting crimes and offences to the prosecutor, and of Force Orders in relation to mentally disturbed offenders, police views and practices vary considerably from area to area. One view was that the prisoner 'belonged to the fiscal' and the charge served as the reason for custody. 'When a person who appears to be mentally disordered has infringed the law, it is the duty of the police to apprehend and detain him in the usual manner', said a senior police officer. One force reported that it did not see its role as *identifying* the mentally abnormal offender and did not wish it to be so. Police in this force viewed their role as one of reporting crime to the procurator fiscal, i.e. the public prosecutor and, should doubts arise as to a person's fitness to be detained in police cells, then the decision of the police surgeon would cover their responsibility until the case reached the procurator fiscal. Should the police surgeon want hospital admission, he would arrange it, but any report given by the police surgeon was a written one in a sealed envelope for the procurator fiscal, not for the police. The attitude of this particular police force may be seen as one of minimal involvement with the individual needs of the detained person and a maximum reliance on passing responsibility to the prosecutor.

By contrast in several other areas the emphasis was on the release of the mentally abnormal person from custody wherever possible, the main concern being to obtain necessary care, even though an offence had been committed. 'The good detective forgets the crime and looks at the individual', a police officer said. Police surgeons in this force gave their reports to the *police* who would in turn advise the procurator fiscal. It was pointed out that local authorities had a commitment to the mentally abnormal under the Social Work (Scotland) Act 1968 and, should a person come into the hands of the police, it was up to the police as agents of the procurator fiscal to take steps to ensure that social work provisions were satisfied in their dealings with a person who was not just an offender, but someone who perhaps as a result of mental disorder had offended.

Differences in interpretation of their role by the police do not occur in a vacuum, but must be considered in the context of the working relationship between procurator fiscal and police. Some police were ready to welcome discussions with procurators fiscal, perhaps leading to a Force Instruction, which would give them guidelines on the information wanted by the fiscals. It is surprising that only in very few areas do any guidelines for processing mentally disordered persons appear to exist.

The research sample

The duty of prosecution of offenders, which in Scotland is undertaken by the procurator fiscal service (see Chapter 4), is laid upon the police in England and Wales and thus working practices develop within one service rather than between two, but the considerations remain similar. Data obtainable from police forces in Scotland may be used to discuss relevant issues. These data were obtained by questionnaires sent to Scottish forces and from discussions held with police officers at levels of policy and practice. Detailed information was obtained on a representative sample of 105 cases where medical advice was sought by police because of suspected mental disturbance in alleged offenders.

It became clear that police policy was translated into practice at a local level mainly by Inspectors responsible for Charge Offices. The Police Inspector interpreted Force Instructions in relation to a particular individual whose behaviour had not only been the subject of a report by his sergeants or constables, but who was physically present. His behaviour and attitudes could be observed. Moreover it was the duty and responsibility of that Inspector to ensure the safe custody of that person over the next few hours or possibly days. Whether or not a person was regarded as mentally ill could depend very much on the individual staff on duty and the circum stances at the time. 'Every case is individual and can only be treated as such within a general framework of local understanding and co-operation between services', said a senior police officer. In particular the police depend on the doctors and it was pointed out that the only persons that the police *knew* were fit to be detained were those whom a doctor had seen and pronounced fit.

John Alderson, writing on the 'demeanour' for policing in *Policing Freedom*[2] makes a clear distinction between policing by an individual and policing in concert by a body of police, and sees the former as demanding and developing superior skills. Although his statement is a general one, the necessity for an immediate response by middle-ranking and junior officers in relation to suspected mentally disordered offenders can be instanced as one example among many of the 'reliance on one's own judgement, discretion and personality' which Alderson claims is normally required in practice. It is not corporate action which is required but an individual decision which has to be made.

How is medical advice sought?

The police duty of reporting crime is coupled with that of ensuring that a person charged is 'not unreasonably and unnecessarily detained in custody'. The purpose of a police request for medical advice is basically to discover whether or not someone is fit to be detained in police custody. How is such advice obtained? In Scotland, other than in City A, advice is obtained from a police surgeon who is usually a general practitioner appointed on a part-time basis for police duties. In some rural areas, general practitioners are called upon, although not formally appointed as police surgeons. One region has a full-time police surgeon but he is not involved in the psychiatric aspect of work. Thus advice on fitness for detention in police hands is given by doctors who are performing a variety of general practice duties in the community as well as for the police. They are not specialists in dealing with mental disorders nor are they qualified under section 27 of the Mental Health (Scotland) Act 1960.

The situation in City A is different. Here a request is passed direct to one of a rota of psychiatrists at the local mental hospital. He is available on a twenty-four hour basis to attend at the police station. His advice is given to the police Inspector; the outcome may be admission to hospital, voluntarily or under section 31 of the Mental Health (Scotland) Act 1960. Unless the psychiatrist recommends immediate hospital admission the person remains in police custody. This system has obvious advantages for the police, who are receiving psychiatric advice as distinct from advice given by a general practitioner. It is also welcomed by the psychiatrists who, at the very beginning of the criminal justice process, are making their own decisions and thereby ensuring that only those patients considered suitable for hospital care are admitted. Thus inappropriate admissions are avoided. For example:

> Female, 52, married, home: breach of the peace: no previous convictions; history of increasing alcohol problems but refused to seek help from family doctor—eventual bout of drinking through night and disturbing neighbours; husband 'phoned police and asked for medical help for her: psychiatrist said 'fit to plead' but should attend own doctor and she promised to do so. Outcome: admonished by the court.

> Male, 22, single; went berserk in his home, throwing furniture and clothing and wardrobe about the house. 'Such behaviour attributed to mentally disturbed person.' Seen by general practitioner at police station, admitted direct to hospital as voluntary patient, no charges preferred. Discharged self from hospital the following day.

There is the further advantage that limited psychiatric information is available for the procurator fiscal with his papers the following morning. However, even where a person is declared fit to be detained, police instructions are such that that person must thereafter be detained until a court appearance the following morning and cannot be released immediately by police.

The situation elsewhere differs. In City B advice on fitness to detain is given by police surgeons, who, by arrangement with the Health Board, can telephone the local mental hospital stating that they are recommending a remand from court to hospital the following day, or need immediate admission with a view to this, and the hospital must admit or find an alternative bed. The police surgeon gives a short written report referring to mental illness and the availability of a bed at the local hospital and this report is received by the procurator fiscal along with the police papers.

The practice is similar in other areas save that the general practitioner/ police surgeon has to find a bed (i.e. it may be his responsibility to *find* rather than the City B practice where the hospital is obliged to *provide* one). Some police, particularly in the more rural areas, commented on difficulties in obtaining hospital beds, but in general the system seemed to the police to be adequate: they were dealing with doctors whom they knew, doctors who were in and out of the police stations for a variety of reasons, and who were often available for informal consultation as a result of this.

Emergency admission under section 31 of the Mental Health (Scotland) Act 1960, that is emergency committal under civil powers, may be recommended by police surgeons, as by all general practitioners, and can be used where immediate admission to hospital from police custody is deemed necessary, although here again the doctor has to find a hospital willing to admit the patient.

From the professional psychiatric point of view, some doctors felt that the system in City B meant at times an inappropriate use of beds, blocking the admission of patients with better claims for treatment. Such decisions on admissions, it was emphasised, were being made by general practitioners with no special experience in psychiatry, and in particular its forensic aspects. In other parts of the country, where the police surgeon/general practitioner system operated and particularly in rural areas, family doctors were much more likely to know the individuals charged, and also to know local psychiatrists, so that informal contacts and exchanges of information took place. In some areas the police reported that in cases of extreme urgency they themselves would take a person direct to the casualty department of a local hospital or the mental hospital itself. For example:

> Male, 27, single. Depressed state on parapet of railway bridge, threatening to throw himself on to line. Removed direct to mental hospital, Section 31 admission, not reported for criminal proceedings.

The source of medical advice and the outcome, where known, for the sample cases are as shown in Table 1.

Of the fifty-six hospital admissions, it was reported that thirty-one were emergency admissions under section 31 Mental Health (Scotland) Act 1960, and fifteen were under voluntary or informal arrangements. In this connection some police criticised the use of what they termed the 'merry-go-round' of voluntary admissions to mental hospitals, especially as they felt that in some cases police or doctors were 'conned' by offenders who, rather than risk a prison sentence, agreed to admission as a voluntary patient, but then walked out of hospital.

TABLE 1

Scotland 1979: Police sample cases: source of medical advice and outcome

	Outcome			
Source of medical advice	Fit to detain in custody	Hospital admission	Other	Total
General practitioner	2	4	2	8
Police surgeon	4	38	3	45
Psychiatrist or Hospital out-patient	11	8	5	24
Other or not known	1	6	21	28
	18	56	31	105

(Figures here and later in the chapter refer to the police sample totalling 105 cases (detailed in Appendix II). Twenty-nine of these cases also appear in the sample from procurators fiscal and/or sheriff clerks—an acceptable figure in that the police total of 404 included 101 such cases and a 1-in-4 sample was attempted.)

Why was medical or specifically psychiatric advice sought?

One police force gave the answer:

1 medical history at Central Records;
2 relatives or accused inform police of recent hospital involvement and police contact hospital;
3 beat police or charge office staff deduce from behaviour;
4 other evidence: the fact that someone does not sober up in cells, bizarre behaviour is reported, violence and destruction continue longer than normal.

Another summed up by saying 'conduct rather than offence is the immediate concern at the police station'.

When the question was also asked for each case in the sample, the reasons given were as shown in Table 2:

TABLE 2

Scotland 1979: Reasons for seeking psychiatric advice: police sample

Bizarre or violent behaviour in committing offence	34
Bizarre or violent behaviour in police hands	11
History of behaviour problems known or reported	11
History of psychiatric problems known or reported	28
General social circumstances	7
Repetition of offending	4
No reason given	10
Total	105

The greatest single cause, noted in almost half the sample cases, was thus violence, i.e. bizarre or violent behaviour either in the offence itself or in police hands thereafter. For example:

Male, 34, single: no previous convictions: ran amok among pedestrians in city centre: psychiatrist reported he was extremely eccentric by nature. Outcome: admonished by the court.

Male, 24: breach of the peace, resisting arrest and vagrancy. Behaved in disorderly manner in the street, conducted himself as a vagrant, resisted arrest, took off all his clothes in police cell, sober. Police noted accused had a previous mental history, having been admitted three times to hospital in the past year, but diagnosed as merely eccentric. Psychiatrist reported fit to detain. Outcome: committal to hospital by the court.

The violence aspect is apparent in the charges preferred against cases in the sample.

TABLE 3

Scotland 1979: Police sample cases where medical/psychiatric advice sought: charges preferred

Charge	Number	% excluding 'not known' cases
Murder	1	1
Serious assault/robbery	4	5
Breach of the peace, petty assault, resisting arrest, offensive weapons	65	72
Property	6	7
Sexual	6	7
Fire-raising	2	2
Other	5	6
Not known	16	—
	105	100

Thus almost three-quarters were offences of breach of the peace or similar, a proportion which is three times as great as that of such charges in the total figure for all crimes and offences in 1979.[3] Of the sixty-five persons so involved, only twelve were known to have no previous convictions, while eleven persons had eleven or more. Twenty-four of the group had previous convictions for minor violence and three for serious crime. Twenty-five of the sixty-five so charged were women and it was obvious that the disturbed female caused considerable problems. For example:

> Female, 50, series of charges over 3 months. *One,* assault and breach of the peace. Under the influence of alcohol. Police surgeon reported no evidence of any psychotic illness. Mental hospital contacted and said fit to detain. *Two,* called at police station, drunk. Advised to call again when sober. Next day, broke windows in public house, arrested while trying to break shop window with her shoe, assaulted police woman when searched. Drunk. Police surgeon said mentally ill, admit to mental hospital, Section 31, for observation. Previously patient there and known to hospital. *Three,* assault and breach of the peace. No indication of any medical reports. Drunk. *Four,* breach of the peace. Police surgeon as in *One* above, drunk, female of low IQ, fit for detention. *Five,* breach of the peace and police assault. No indication of any medical reports, drunk, detained.

It should be remembered that as well as the use of a breach of the peace charge to cover a very wide range of behaviour, it can also be used as a means of obtaining access to medical help for the socially inadequate.

In every police force a recurring problem was that of violent behaviour by persons in custody. It was pointed out that only the police saw cases 'hot' and often extreme violence was over (or ceased immediately) when medical help arrived. In some instances when they were asked to detain someone in custody the police felt that the very sight of uniforms and the locking of cell doors increased violence. For example:

> Male, 16, single, home: absconder from list D school who went berserk when police went to his home—smashed furniture, broke window, fought all the way to the police car, fought in hospital casualty department and refused medical attention to cut hand—long police statement re history of violent and anti-social behaviour: police surgeon said quiet to point of morosity when examined some hours later. Outcome: 3 months' Detention Centre.

The problem raised by police in many discussions was that they were left to handle those persons 'whom the hospitals didn't want . . . the violent alcoholic, the disruptive female . . . the personality disorders . . .'. To quote from one case, 'the police surgeon attempted to have her admitted to the local mental hospital . . . it transpired that as soon as the hospital staff knew the identity of the potential patient they point-blank refused to permit her admission'. It was felt that such persons were not only difficult to contain and placed a considerable responsibility on the police, but that they also made a very large demand on scarce police resources. Constant supervision in a police cell could mean the use of two officers per shift over an entire weekend if, as in some city areas, an offender had to be moved to a police station which had observation cells. In areas without such facilities a fifteen-minute check appeared to be normal practice, but it was pointed out that full twenty-four hour surveillance was not possible. For example:

> Female, 23, single, home: breach of the peace: 2 previous convictions for breach of the peace, assaulted mother and sister in epileptic fit, they sent for police who apprehended her for her own safety but so violent when they attempted to put her in cell that she was kept in waiting room under observation: family doctor to police station—stated she needed psychiatric treatment but he had no facilities to have her admitted to hospital: social worker attempted to have her admitted to place of care but without success: police surgeon arranged emergency admission to hospital under Section 31.

The police view was that pressure to contain the violent or dangerous offender was placed on them from both medical and criminal justice sources—both from the hospitals who did not admit, and from procurators fiscal who, when consulted about serious crime or when an element of danger was involved, might naturally prefer the physical security of police custody to the open hospital ward (see Chapter 4). For example:

> Male, 50, single, no fixed abode, unemployed. Seen by police carrying strips of metal, said he had stolen them. Appeared to be of unsound mind in police station. Police rang hospital and found he had been discharged two weeks previously. Hospital not prepared to have him back, as prior to discharge he was examined and found to be of sound mind. Accused now ranting, bawling, hallucinated in police station. Police surgeon sent for, man admitted under Section 31. Police surgeon reports indicate this man seen two weeks previously in another police office, and then considered fit to plead but 'marked deterioration in his mental state since then'. Outcome: no proceedings on charge of theft, as requested by police in their report.

In one town, for instance, despite the good relationship with the local mental hospital, it was noted that violent cases, even if mentally disordered, might have to be detained by the police on a twenty-four hour watch. Only a forensic psychiatry unit in one city hospital appeared to offer security acceptable to police and prosecution. On the other hand, it must be acknowledged that violent behaviour is not necessarily a medical matter, and the detention of the alleged offender who exhibits violent behaviour may properly be the responsibility of the police.

The next most common reason for seeking medical advice was a history of psychiatric problems in the alleged offender. On-the-spot information from a suspect or his family or friends was the usual source of such data. But a very wide variation was reported by police in the quality and quantity of such information from official sources. In City A, a request for psychiatric advice always resulted in a red 'M.H.' (mental health) warning signal being entered on a police record, whatever the outcome of such advice. It is not normal for the advice of a police surgeon to be so noted in other forces, and where the procurator fiscal marks a case 'no proceedings' because of the medical report no record will reach the Scottish Criminal

Records Office. Furthermore information may not reach the appropriate records before another charge, e.g. another breach of the peace a week later. In City B, a warning signal is carried on criminal records to denote violence or dangerousness (e.g. carrying of weapons) but not mental illness.

There may be twenty-four hour availability of a check on police records, but other records, e.g. hospital, are not so readily accessible. In some instances information is recorded where 'crimes' are concerned but not for the less serious category of 'offences'. The computerisation of police records which is currently proposed may mean that much 'soft' information is lost in future. Hospital admissions are not noted unless they result from a Court Order (eight in the sample had such a record) and here the ethics of disclosing medical information may be a problem. If police in the course of their investigations become aware of personal medical information, should this be recorded? If police in the course of their investigations seek information from a mental hospital, should such information be disclosed? There were wide regional differences on these matters, and the subject of ethics and attitudes is not for discussion here, although it is worth noting the recommendation of the Butler Committee[4] that 'where it comes to light in the course of court proceedings that a defendant has received psychiatric treatment a note should be made in the police records of the name of the hospital concerned and the dates when treatment was carried out, if known'. It became apparent that considerable gaps in information were present and that parallel careers in the medical and criminal justice worlds were possible, and occasionally the existence of each might be unknown to the other.

The third set of reasons may be regarded as broadly social: personal circumstances, and previous history of offending. The age and sex breakdown of the sample is shown in Table 4:

TABLE 4

Scotland 1979: Age and sex of cases where psychiatric advice sought by police

Age	Under 17	17–20	21–30	31–50	51 & over	Not known	Total
M	3	7	17	31	13	3	74
F	—	3	8	15	5	—	31
Total	3	10	25	46	18	3	105

Twenty-nine were married or cohabiting but forty were single, separated or divorced; fifty-four were unemployed; twenty were of no fixed abode; in thirty-three cases alcohol was involved at the time of the crime or offence;

fifty-one were known to have previous convictions. From these data can be deduced the police involvement in dealing with the inadequate petty offender, described by one force as the 'settled vagrants' of the city centres, where the police are filling a gap in social services. Medical attention may be difficult to obtain for such persons, and a breach of the peace charge may be a gateway through which to bring help. For example:

> Male, 17, single: indecent assault (attempts to embrace female students in dark street): no previous convictions: police reported low intellect and needing psychiatric help but also home conditions as poor—no heating, lighting, cooking facilities. Outcome: 18 months' probation with condition of attendance for out-patient psychiatric treatment.

Once again (as with those violent in custody) police drew attention to the utilisation of police resources and police time to deal with the socially inadequate. Scarce resources were diverted away from dealing with serious crime and crime prevention.

Police reasons for seeking psychiatric advice have been summarised above into the three categories of behaviour, history and social characteristics and this is a pattern which could be applied, with minor and understandable variations, to reasons given for seeking similar advice in prosecution and court processes as Chapters 4 and 5 will show.

Informal police action

Whereas the information discussed above relates to cases handled formally within the police system, it is the lot of every police officer in carrying out his duties to be called upon to exercise considerable discretion, not least in relation to members of the public whose mental state may bring them to the notice of authority. Information was therefore sought on the 'grey area' between those cases where a charge was made and those where help or advice was sought for a mentally abnormal person or where a situation was handled without any formal charge being made.

As well as their duty where the law is broken, the general police duty 'to protect life and property' may involve them in dealing with mentally disordered persons. Indeed the general public has a habit of looking to the police as the visible source of help in almost any situation. This is borne out by the many instances reported which originated in a family situation where the police were the immediate source of help in an emergency often involving violent or disturbed behaviour. For example:

> Male, 48, married, home: breach of the peace: 19 previous convictions; had axe in hand and asked son to call doctor as he felt depressed—son could not get doctor—man went berserk and smashed furniture: long history of drink and violence, former in-patient treatment and currently out-patient: police surgeon said he had failed to keep a hospital appointment that day and arranged Section 31

admission. Police comment—'when he is sober he revels in the fact that he can convince doctors he requires psychiatric treatment . . . period of imprisonment to act as drying out period would be of more benefit to X and his family than psychiatric treatment at the hospital.'

Female, 29, single, no fixed abode: breach of the peace: no previous convictions, 18 years in mental hospital, discharged to family home, created disturbance same day, not welcome and warned to leave area, shouting, swearing, etc., in common stair—hospital declined to readmit: psychiatric report stated fit to plead and appear in court. Outcome: 2 years' probation.

Police officers spoke of two types of case:

1) where a minor charge did not need to be pursued because medical help was available, for example:

Male, 58, married, home: Contrary Post Office Act 1969, Section 78: no previous convictions: 'phoned 999 saying he had been shot—wife told of medical treatment earlier in day: police surgeon arranged voluntary hospital admission and police reported he was receiving treatment and unlikely to be discharged for several weeks;

and

2) where a minor charge was made deliberately because medical help was *not* available in any other way.

The former occurred particularly in the neighbourhood of large mental hospitals to which patients were returned by police, for example, after petty disturbances or minor shoplifting. In the latter the culprits were often socially inadequate rather than mentally ill and were thus not acceptable in mental hospitals. Police felt in some instances that psychiatrists were so used to seeing the extremes of mental illness that they did not take any notice of the 'ordinary' mental case and made it difficult for the police to obtain medical help for them.

It could be argued that the particular gate used to obtain medical help does not matter so long as help is obtained. However, the use of the criminal justice gateway can have long-term and serious implications for the individual, particularly for those with no previous convictions who face a criminal charge—for example for breach of the peace following a minor disturbance—because medical help was not available by any other route. Likewise a petty recidivist could face a long loss of liberty in a hospital which might be seen as out of all proportion to what is merely another breach of the peace. Such a responsibility the police may have to accept, although the decision as to how an incident is handled is largely forced on them by the particular practices or administrative procedures of other services in the area in which they work.

Police practices and the extent of reporting vary so much from force to force that the extent of their informal contact with the mentally abnormal cannot be quantified. But some limited calculation of numbers was possible for City C which is unique in possessing a forensic psychiatric unit, enabling police in that City to use section 104 of the Mental Health (Scotland) Act 1960 (the only force routinely to do so). By this means persons thought to be mentally disordered, in a place to which the public have access, may be removed to a hospital and detained for treatment. Further information on contacts with the mentally abnormal in 1979 were provided by various police divisions. One division noted some one hundred incidents which involved the police when neither an information nor an offence report was submitted, and included missing persons, suicides or attempted suicides, and 'unharmful but peculiar behaviour causing concern to the public or the police', about half being patients from the local mental hospital. Police in another division recalled thirty-one cases, many involving mental patients, but could not give a total for the year. It was apparent that all police forces had a great deal of contact with local mental hospitals and that many good relationships of mutual advantage had developed. Also it was noted that suicides and para-suicides (some with consequent 999 ambulance calls) made frequent demands on police time.

While it was not possible on the basis of the present research study to give a figure for the number of informal police contacts with members of the public who may be mentally disturbed, there is nevertheless strong evidence that such duties take up a considerable part of police time.

Police/medical service relationship

It was also apparent that contacts between police and medical services were not always entirely harmonious. Mention has been made of the police feeling that the violent who may have offended are left on their hands. Two cases follow, selected at random from police reports, but many more instances were quoted:

A 33-year-old man with a history of mental illness created a serious disturbance within his home when he used violence towards his parents by presenting an axe at them and threatened to kill them. The police were summoned and attended at the locus. The man was disarmed and after considerable persuasion he eventually calmed down. His family doctor was contacted but showed little interest and declined to attend. The following morning the man appeared at Sheriff Court and pled guilty to charges of assault and Breach of the Peace. He was remanded for Psychiatric Report.

32-year-old male, an informal patient of a hospital clinic, suffering from mental illness, caused a disturbance in his home occupied by his widowed mother. Subject removed from his home to the local police station. The clinic contacted but refused to admit. Duty Social Worker contacted and refused to attend at Police Station. Subject released from Police custody and allowed to walk the street. About three months later after this incident, subject was eventually certified under Section 31 of the Mental Health (Scotland) Act, 1960, and admitted to hospital.

In both examples the situation may have been correctly handled from a medical point of view: what is of concern is that the police did not feel that this was so.

It seems that many such cases are due to a lack of understanding between the services—a lack of knowledge by the police of current medical and psychiatric thinking and practice, particularly in relation to the open-door policy of mental hospitals. A number of police officers thought there was a need for a much greater provision of maximum security hospital beds.

The policeman faced with a responsibility he feels unfit or unable to shoulder, or who feels that to shoulder it is to add unfairly to his own varied and heavy load, is seeking to shift the burden of responsibility to where he feels it more properly belongs. The psychiatrist implementing a policy of open wards, faced with demands for scarce beds, not willing to admit a patient whom he cannot treat, is not sympathetic to the police demands nor appreciative of the pressures in a busy police station.

The police/medical service relationship is not a formalised one as is that of police/procurator fiscal, and there seems to be a need for intercommunication to promote the understanding necessary for informal working to develop. Allowance has not only to be made for the differing day-to-day duties, responsibilities and stresses of both services, but also for the fundamental differences between police, as part of a criminal justice system based on order, law and an adversarial approach, and psychiatry dealing as it does with an individual, his thinking and his needs.[5]

Police/social work relationship

It was not possible to study the role of the social worker, but it was obvious that between the attitudes of police and social worker the gap was usually considerable.

In City A the practice of direct recourse by police to psychiatrist was adopted because it was not possible to appoint designated mental health officers at the time of the implementation of the Social Work (Scotland) Act 1968. In City B there are mental health officers in each area team, but the emergency number, available on a twenty-four hour basis to the police, is directed to a duty officer who may in turn have to locate a mental health officer. Again, in some rural areas there were complaints of the inaccessibility of social workers due to distance and to duty hours, but in others reliance was placed on the known social worker who obviously was part of the community network of care. In general the police experience as reported was that they themselves provided the only real twenty-four hour service of social help. The communication gap here appears to be a wider one than that separating them from the medical services.[6]

Comment

Police exercise of discretion in relation to mental abnormality has been described in terms of lay decision-making based on expediency, but it is not an exercise complete in itself: it is one part of the duty of reporting to the procurator fiscal which occurs under the overall umbrella of the formal police-procurator fiscal working relationship. This will be considered in the next chapter. What must be emphasised here is the vital role of the police not only as operating the gateway to the criminal justice system and hence influencing or limiting subsequent stages, but also in dealing direct with the alleged offenders. The police see 'the body': initially the procurator fiscal normally sees only written reports.

Chapter 4

The Prosecution Process

Between the maintenance of order of the executive and the administration of law of the judiciary, the two distinct aspects of the maintenance of law and order, lies the 'shadowy region' where decisions are made about prosecution. Prosecution must be impartial, but should not be indiscriminate. It is therefore important to see where in principle and in practice the responsibility for prosecution lies.

In principle in England and Wales, as distinct from Scotland, every citizen has a right or even a duty to bring a prosecution; in practice (although precise figures are not available) the right is little exercised. The question of a public prosecution service has been one of debate in greater or lesser degree for centuries. It led to the Prosecution of Offences Act in 1879 which created the office of Director of Public Prosecutions, an official empowered to deal directly with a limited amount of serious criminal behaviour, but to do no more than advise police forces on the initiation of proceedings regarding the bulk of such behaviour. The right of private prosecution remained, but most prosecutions have been initiated by the legal departments of regional police forces. Current debate led to the Philips Report[1] which after referring to the accusatorial nature of the trial dictating the nature of the pre-trial process, emphasised the fundamental need for balance between the interest of the community and the rights and liberties of the individual, and went on to consider prosecution in detail. The proposal finally presented on grounds of consistency, accountability and efficiency was that of a legally based statutory prosecution service (a Crown Prosecutor) with responsibility for prosecution proceedings in court once the initial decision to proceed has been taken by the police. The right to private prosecution would remain, with application in the first instance to the Crown Prosecutor.[2]

In Scotland private prosecution virtually ended in 1587 when the Lord Advocate was empowered to conduct criminal prosecutions in the name of the Crown. Since 1907 the procurator fiscal, formerly the investigating officer of the Sheriff, has been under the control of the Lord Advocate and has become the prosecuting official, i.e. the public prosecutor. The investigation of crime is in practical terms in the hands of the police and section 17 of the Police (Scotland) Act 1967 states '. . . it shall be the duty of the constables of a police force . . . where an offence has been committed . . . to make such reports to the appropriate prosecutor as may be necessary for the purpose of bringing the offender with all due speed to justice . . . to take every precaution to ensure that any person charged with an offence is not unreasonably and unnecessarily detained in custody . . . the chief constable shall comply with such lawful instructions as he may receive from the appropriate prosecutor'.

Thus although the underlying purpose of prosecution is the same north and south of the border the practicalities in England differ from those in Scotland. The police service in England currently combines the duties of both investigation and prosecution. The distinctions, referred to in the earlier chapter concerning the police (pp. 17 *et seq.*) between expediency and justice, between lay and professional, may therefore become blurred, but they do not necessarily disappear if conditions in England and Wales are examined.

Discussion which follows in this chapter takes a practical view of the role of the procurator fiscal, the public prosecutor, in Scotland. His method of functioning raises issues of principle and practice which are common to prosecution in both legal systems, as did the earlier discussion on the investigative and reporting role of the police. In neither the English nor the Scottish judicial system does prosecution automatically follow from knowledge that a person has committed an offence. If that person is mentally disordered then such disorder is a relevant fact to be taken into account at the time of prosecution. Indeed the procurator fiscal has a statutory obligation in this matter as defined in sections 175 and 376 of the Criminal Procedure (Scotland) Act 1975 which specifically state: '(2) Where it appears to the procurator in any court before which a person is charged with an offence that the person may be suffering from mental disorder, it shall be the duty of such prosecutor to bring before the court such evidence as may be available of the mental condition of that person.'

Whoever in fact makes the decision to prosecute, the administrative framework in which he acts, and the degree of his personal responsibility in decision-making are of importance not only to the alleged offender, but also to society. The criminal law must be seen to be consistently applied, must not be seen to be brought into disrepute by unsuccessful prosecutions, must not be seen to be applied harshly. In practice the first step is the making of a formal charge by a police officer. This function of a police officer of relatively junior rank—station sergeant or inspector—in deciding whether or not to accept a charge following arrest, although made according to strict instructions or guidelines, is an important area of the use of discretion in decision-making.[3] In England and Wales the use of discretion, where it exists, in subsequent decisions as to sufficiency of evidence, the need to prosecute, the exact nature of the charge and the appropriate court in which to proceed remains in the hands of police forces. Responsibility rests with the Chief Superintendent of a division, who will refer to his legal department those cases which are prosecuted in the higher courts where counsel must be briefed and also those cases where he needs legal advice. Although the decision-makers may perchance be lawyers, the vast amount of routine decision-making is carried out by people acting in their capacity as police officers.

In Scotland all these subsequent decisions are in the hands of the procurator fiscal, no matter how petty the offence, and all procurators fiscal are professionally qualified lawyers acting in a legal capacity. Once a formal charge has been made there is an end to police discretion: the case must go to the procurator fiscal and police procedures are wholly administrative to this end. The procurator fiscal decides on the sufficiency of evidence, the necessity of prosecution, the nature of the charge and the appropriate court.[4] Cases of more serious crime to be prosecuted on indictment in the higher courts are processed through the Lord Advocate's Department (the Crown Office) and led in court by advocates depute (i.e. barristers).

But, each procurator fiscal being autonomous, and with so much discretion in the hands of individual fiscals, in Scotland there could be room for as much disparity in law enforcement as there is between the separate police forces in England and Wales. In neither jurisdiction is it customary to make public the reasons for a decision not to prosecute in any particular case.

It was noted earlier that the elements of lay *versus* professional decision-making, and of expediency *versus* criminal justice were relevant in the context of prosecution. Thus, the police were categorised as making a lay decision in the context of expediency. The procurator fiscal, however, stands as a professional making a decision in criminal justice terms. The police decision was seen as one of a series each possibly based on differing criteria, whereas the professional status of the procurator fiscal provides him with fixed criteria upon which all his decision-making takes place. Perhaps more importantly the police were seen to be dealing with the person in a real and practical sense—what he is; the procurator fiscal is initially dealing with what is reported to him about that person and his alleged offending—what he has done. But the procurator fiscal is totally dependent on the police in order to carry out his own assigned duties, and these seeming opposites combine to form the key of interdependence which opens the gate into the formal criminal justice process. In broad terms the police duty in Scotland can be summed up as that of collecting and providing information, whereas the procurator fiscal remit is to decide on what has been set before him.

There are other differences between the two decisions, one of circumstances and one of outlook. The police decision is a practical one often made under pressure of time; the procurator fiscal's decision is one of principle with time for consideration. The police officer is making a personal and individualistic decision, his judgement usually ruled by expediency; the procurator fiscal is viewing crime (and the mental state of the criminal) from a legal and societal point of view. In practice of course the two services work closely together and the police carry out their investigative role according to the instruction of the procurator fiscal. Local levels of understanding useful in relation to petty offending and to local needs are an asset to the police and the procurator fiscal is available to give advice or to give authority or to be present at investigations of a serious nature. Indeed he always attends when the case is one of murder.

Each procurator fiscal in Scotland is making his own decisions on individual cases, but the pattern of decision-making focuses in turn on the deed itself—whether the behaviour as described constitutes a crime and, if so, whether evidence is available to substantiate the charge—and then on the consequences of prosecution—whether the deed warrants or requires prosecution. Renton and Brown,[5] the standard textbook on Scottish criminal procedure, sets out the tests to be applied when considering prosecution thus:

1 whether the facts disclosed in the information constitute either a crime according to the common law of Scotland, or a contravention of an Act of Parliament which extends to that country;
2 whether there is sufficient evidence in support of these facts to justify the institution of criminal proceedings;
3 whether the act or omission charged is of sufficient importance to be made the subject of a criminal prosecution;
4 whether there is any reason to suspect that the information is inspired by malice or ill-will on the part of the informant towards the person charged;
5 whether there is sufficient excuse for the conduct of the accused person to warrant the abandonment of proceedings against him;
6 whether the case is more suitable for trial in the civil court, in respect that the facts raise a question of civil right.

Test 5 can clearly include mental disorder, and at the later stages of decision-making as noted above the question of mental disorder is relevant not only for the alleged offender, but also for the general public. It would be difficult to argue in favour of the worth or the need of prosecution in relation to petty shoplifting or disorderly behaviour by a mentally disordered patient from a local mental hospital, but equally it would be difficult or indeed impossible not to prosecute if the offence was serious assault where the intervention of the law would be required for the protection of the community.

There is a tendency, when mental disorder is mentioned along with criminal justice, to think immediately of murder cases, of insanity pleas, of diminished responsibility, of special hospitals and of life sentences. In fact not only are murder charges few[6] in number in relation to the volume of law-breaking passing through the criminal justice system, but there are procedures which ensure that evidence relating to the mental state of those accused of murder is routinely considered. In Scotland, as in England, the request for reports from two psychiatrists is automatic. It is, however, in relation to much less serious offending that matters concerning mental disorder are more frequent and more problematic as the Scottish study shows.

The view has been expressed by some procurators fiscal that their concern in recent years, stemming from earlier psychiatric thought and teaching, has been towards more abstract concepts of responsibility when considering how far the mental state of an offender should be taken into account. The question asked has tended to be whether an offender is ill, and, if ill, whether he needs treatment: a tendency for the concern to move from punishment-and-treatment to treatment of itself. But two points tend to be overlooked if the treatment aspect is over-emphasised. One is that 'once mentally ill' does not necessarily mean 'always mentally ill', and the other, again in colloquial terms, that 'mad' *and.*'bad' is possible.[7] Within this wide framework there is considerable variety among procurators fiscal in views of their own role. The decision to call for a psychiatric report is a subjective one on the part of the fiscal marking papers. At one extreme there is the limited view that part of the fiscal remit is simply to gain information on the point of 'sane and fit to plead', rather than to give any consideration to the possible medical need of the accused person, and that the chief responsibility is with the crime and not the criminal. At the other extreme there are a number of fiscals who feel strongly, not only that medical advice leading to treatment might be necessary, but who wish to see some system of getting such psychiatric information or advice without even the necessity of a court appearance which normally requires at least one night in police custody for an arrested person. At the time of writing, in one Scottish city, police can routinely and directly obtain a psychiatric opinion at any time of the day or night concerning any person held in custody. Elsewhere such advice is normally only possible in emergencies, and police routinely seek advice instead from general practitioners or part-time police surgeons. The procurator fiscal cannot order a psychiatric report without bringing the offender before the court. Thus not only are procurators fiscal dependent on the police to alert them to the possible need for a psychiatric report, but the only possibility of papers being marked 'no proceedings' without a court appearance in the case of a mentally abnormal person is when police alert the fiscal to the appropriate information.

Most procurators fiscal stress their reliance on the police, and their own willingness to act on information given: instances were quoted where 'no proceedings' decisions had been made. For example, one procurator fiscal commented that, if hospital action had already been taken, then a case might be marked 'no proceedings' and the individual left to be dealt with through the Mental Health Services. He instanced a girl of eighteen who had abducted a child: her own general practitioner arranged her admission from police custody to a mental hospital (where she had received treatment before) under Section 31 of the Mental Health (Scotland) Act 1960. Since she accepted the treatment situation, no proceedings were taken. Minor charges of breach of the peace or petty assault in family circumstances could be similarly handled. One procurator fiscal wrote to a psychiatrist— 'You are prepared to deal with this man without reference to court . . . any proceedings are now at an end.' On the other hand, one procurator fiscal made it clear that he himself would never mark a case 'no proceedings' simply because of reported mental problems.

The question of calling for reports also depends on a procurator fiscal's own view of mental hospitals—as 'prison'? as 'punishment'? as 'care'? as 'cure'? Some view the loss of liberty involved in compulsory hospitalisation as too heavy a penalty for minor offending and are reluctant to invoke psychiatrists in every possible case. They are aware of the dilemma concerning an offender whose mental abnormality might have no connection with his offending and yet who is placed, perhaps unwillingly, in a treatment situation as a result of it.

Binns *et al.*[8] reporting on admissions to Leverndale in the mid 1960s, state: 'Their offence was the means whereby attention was drawn to their mental ill-health and had the effect of rendering treatment obligatory rather than optional.' But psychiatric treatment as a result of a court appearance is a chance thing, a haphazard way of dealing with a possible need for treatment if indeed such need is to be reckoned as of importance. It was also pointed out that either the guilty could slip through the administration's meshes or the innocent could be incarcerated in hospital, if medical needs alone were considered.

The research sample[9]

As was done with referrals by the police in Scotland, so an attempt was made to discover routines, reasons and results where psychiatric reports were sought by procurators fiscal. The questions of who first queries the mental state of an accused person, at what stage in the criminal proceedings, and at what stage in an offender's career this takes place are all important questions. The dependence of the procurators fiscal on police information to alert them to the need for seeking psychiatric advice was continually stressed. It was pointed out that if there was no such prompting from police, nor from a defence solicitor, then it was unlikely that a procurator fiscal himself would initiate the request for a psychiatric report. There may, however, be no comment concerning mental abnormality in a police report and no indication of special circumstances at first court appearance. A defence solicitor might not report that he is unable to get coherent instructions from an accused until immediately before a trial. In these circumstances some mentally abnormal offenders could slip through the net.

Reference is made in Chapter 5 to the differing practices in courts. In some areas all psychiatric reports for the courts are generated by the procurator fiscal whether wanted by himself before plea, or by the sheriff clerk before sentence. In other areas reports wanted by the sheriff to assist him with regard to sentence are organised by the sheriff clerk himself. The routines described below in relation to procurators fiscal may therefore refer to reports sought at one or other of these two stages in the criminal justice process. The information was derived from discussions with procurators fiscal representing each fiscal region and from the questionnaires completed in relation to 228 cases in the procurator fiscal sample.

Routines

As with any organisation pressed for time, and liable to increasing postal delays, much of the detail of psychiatric reports for the courts is initiated by telephone to be followed by written confirmation which varies considerably in form and content. The general pattern is that of a telephone call to an administrator or secretary at the appropriate hospital or clinic (according to health board catchment areas) giving basic information on name, address, charge, whether remanded in prison or ordained to appear, and the date of next court appearance. The medical arrangements thereafter are a matter of hospital or clinic working practices, but there is considerable variation in the written confirmation sent by procurators fiscal. Some requests are addressed to a named psychiatrist who will do the report, others to the Physician Superintendent who is asked to arrange it. What were psychiatrists told about the case and what were they asked to provide?

Which psychiatrist?

Throughout most of Scotland there is little choice in who is asked, in that the request is to the (appropriate doctor in the) nearest mental hospital. Although the reluctance of some psychiatrists to be involved in forensic work was mentioned, there did not seem to be a problem in obtaining reports in principle: problems were more often in relation to the practicalities of travelling to see the defendant and ensuring the report was available within the allotted time. The status and place of work of the psychiatrist reporting could be of importance in the sense that a consultant has control over admissions to his own beds but not over admission to anyone else's.[10]

What was told and what was asked?

There was wide variation in the amount of information made available to psychiatrists, and considerable discussion as to how much should in fact be given. Was it to be assumed that the accused was guilty? In some instances police reports were given to the doctors, in others a summary of the reports. Sometimes there were telephone discussions between procurators fiscal and psychiatrists. Psychiatrists felt that a description of the offence together with an account of behaviour at the time of arrest and after imprisonment was crucial to the understanding of a case.[11] Chapter V, para. 71, of the Report on Forensic Psychiatry (Scottish Health Services Council, October 1968: The Harper Report) recommended sending information about the offence, especially as there was direct communication between procurator fiscal and psychiatrist. Para. 180(4) of the Criminal Procedure (Scotland) Act 1975 states that 'the court shall send a statement of the reasons for which the court is of opinion that an inquiry ought to be made . . . ' after plea or finding of guilt.

What was being asked seemed frequently to be assumed: in the sample of 228 cases a clear request as to fitness to plead was specified in twenty-nine (thirteen per cent) cases, but no clear reason at all was noted in 149 (sixty-five per cent). In fact confusion as to the purpose of the psychiatric report was likely because of this omission. If the request is from the procurator fiscal for his own purpose, then advice on fitness to plead may be required; if the request is from the procurator fiscal on behalf of the sheriff clerk, then the need may be for a recommendation for disposal. Some reports were in the form of (a) an opinion on fitness to plead followed by (b) a recommendation for disposal should guilt or mental disorder be established, but only sixteen of the 182 (nine per cent) psychiatric reports seen mentioned the specific purpose for which they had been requested. Some procurator fiscal offices sent copies of a printed form which gave the psychiatrist a clear indication of the purpose of the report. It may be that procurators fiscal are themselves unsure of what they seek, indeed it was said that 'to get a psychiatric report is a good holding situation for a fiscal'.

Reasons in principle

What is asked of the psychiatrist clearly depends on why it is asked. Is the fiscal looking simply for a decision on fitness to plead, or is he looking for guidance on the wider issue of how best to discover and serve the medical needs of the defendant? The response to a report indicating fitness to plead but also suggesting possible mental disorder could well vary according to who reads it. But the issue is not straight cut: the crime itself must be taken into account, as well as the nature of any mental abnormality which is reported. A severely mentally ill defendant who had committed a minor crime, which represented no risk to the public, might escape prosecution if the procurator fiscal was satisfied that suitable arrangements were made for the person's care.

The Butler Committee in considering relief from prosecution summarised its position thus:

> Where any apparent offender is clearly in urgent need of psychiatric treatment and there is *no question of risk to members of the public* the question should always be asked whether any useful public purpose would be served by prosecution (our italics);

and it goes on to state:

> these remarks apply in cases of homicide or attempted homicide or grave bodily harm as in less serious cases.

Thus the risk of violence, or danger to the public, must always be counter-weights to medical need—the conflict between the needs of the individual and the rights of the community is found here as elsewhere in the criminal justice system. Translated into practical terms, the questions of serious crime, and in particular risks of violence, appear to weight the balance in favour of public protection measures in the early stages of the process. Where serious crimes are concerned, the police forces stress that it is necessary at the direction of the procurator fiscal that the offender, even if mentally disordered, be kept in custody. However, consultation with the procurators fiscal on a twenty-four hour basis made early transfer to hospital possible in some cases. This is mainly a question of security—the seriousness of the crime as well as violence necessitating police custody whatever the medical considerations. Only in one city was it reported that Criminal Investigation Department men might take the offender direct to the psychiatric forensic unit because they had confidence in the unit's ability to produce him in court the next morning. In another city it was stated that the procurator fiscal preferred that cases should go to hospital *from* court, save in emergency, so ensuring that the court retained its authority over the individual.

When a case reached court, the question of dangerousness or violence in those remanded for psychiatric reports was again an issue. Procurators fiscal did not all seem aware of the limited degree of security which is found in mental hospitals, or indeed that a secure ward meant secure by medical and nursing standards but not by prison standards. Most hospitals have arrangements to provide security appropriate for patients by a combination of physical means and staffing levels, but a hospital is not primarily a secure establishment.

Reasons in practice

Before considering court routines, it is pertinent to consider what factors prompt the request for psychiatric advice. What in fact are the reasons for psychiatric involvement? This question was asked for all the sample cases and the answers received for 162 of the 228 cases are summarised in Table 1:

TABLE 1

Scotland 1979: Procurator fiscal reasons for requesting psychiatric reports

	Number	%
Nature of offence	56	35
Bizarre behaviour in relation to offending	21	13
History of psychiatric involvement or behavioural problems	32	20
Previous court order to hospital	3	2
Information from defence	4	2
Alcohol	20	12
Murder	26	16
	162	100

Reports in murder cases are routinely obtained and if these are excluded then fifty-seven per cent of reports were sought because of the nature of the offence *per se* or because of behaviour in relation to it, and a further twenty-six per cent because of a past history of psychiatric treatment.

Police reasons were summarised as violence, personal history and social circumstances. Procurator fiscal reasons can be seen as the offence, personal history and social circumstances.

The crimes and offences charged for the sample groups are shown in Table 2:

TABLE 2

Scotland 1979: Crimes and offences where psychiatric reports requested by procurators fiscal and by police

	Procurator fiscal		Police	
	Number	*%*	*Number*	*%*
Murder	26	11	1	1
Serious assault, robbery	11	5	4	4
Breach of the peace, assault	82	36	65	62
Property	45	20	6	6
Road Traffic	10	4	—	—
Drugs	2	—	—	—
Sexual	31	14	1	6
Fire-raising	8	4	2	2
Other	13	6	18	18
	228	100	105	100

Police, dealing with the immediate situation, are less concerned with the nature of the offence and more with exhibited behaviour. The court might seek advice concerning the sex offender or housebreaker or indeed murderer who may have been docile in police custody: the violent man in the cells may be docile and present no problem in court. This can be clearly seen if the charges concerned in the two groups are compared, and is particularly apparent in cases of breach of the peace and petty assaults. This group of people caused immediate police problems in sixty-two per cent of cases and only accounted for thirty-six per cent of fiscal cases, although even this latter figure is significantly larger than the seventeen per cent of persons proceeded against on such charges (*1979 Criminal Statistics (Scotland)*). The use of the breach of the peace charge to cover a very wide variety of circumstances has already been noted, and, of the eighty-two such cases in the fiscal sample, unusual or quasi-medical circumstances were noted in fifty-nine. These included such cases as the following:

Male, 20, single: Breach of the peace and indecent assault—'voices told him to'.

Male, 24, married: Breaches of the peace—'phoning or visiting women pretending to be a doctor doing medical research'.

Female, 28, married: Breach of the peace—drinking and threatened to cut wrists.

Male, 19, single: Breach of the peace and careless driving—stabbed himself in the abdomen.

Male, 33, single: no fixed abode: Breach of the peace—returned to lodgings drunk, 'living in fantasy world'.

Male, 28, single: Breach of the peace—although sober went berserk in house.

Female, 23, separated: Breach of the peace—had drinks, claimed she was 'possessed by the devil'.

Male, 17, single: Breach of the peace—glue sniffing.

Two psychiatric reports were always requested in cases of murder, and there seemed to be general agreement among procurators fiscal that advice should be sought concerning offenders in sexual offences and in fire-raising. Although psychiatrists now state they have little to offer in the way of compulsory treatment for the sex offender, the courts continue to seek advice on the degree of public danger as well as on the medical needs or condition of an accused. Again the conflict of individual need and community protection is apparent.

Both services were concerned when a history of psychiatric or behavioural problems came to light, and here in particular the fiscal service is dependent on information from the police—information contained in the police report of the incident, or information in police records (see Chapter 3) alerting the courts to a medical history. (An attempt was made to note the information psychiatrists had available to them when preparing reports and in over fifty per cent of the cases reference was made by the psychiatrist to previous medical history.)

The third type of reasons has already been noted in the police sample, namely the social-personal circumstances and previous convictions. For example:

Female, 52, widow. No previous convictions. Charge: Assault. Minor altercation with neighbours. Deaf mute living in squalid conditions. Poor eyesight, markedly mentally retarded. Informal admission to hospital recommended until social help can be arranged. Outcome: admonished.

Male, 17, single. No previous convictions. Charge: Lewd and libidinous practices (4- and 7-old girls). Police report as mentally handicapped. Mother has been an in-patient in mental hospital. Social work efforts to secure supervision for him unsuccessful. Psychiatric report states mentally defective and incapable of an independent life. A danger to others when not supervised. Recommend: Probation with an in-patient treatment. Outcome: as per recommendation.

The age and sex distribution of the fiscal sample is shown in Table 3:

TABLE 3

Scotland 1979: Age and sex of offenders for whom psychiatric reports requested by procurators fiscal

	Under 17	17–20	21–30	31–50	51 & over	not known	Total
M	9	52	47	67	14	1	190
F	—	5	11	16	6	—	38
Total	9	57	58	83	20	1	228

This sex ratio of 5:1 should be compared with the ratio for all crimes and offences which is 9:1. The 31–50 age group is over-represented in this sample in comparison with all offenders. Sixty-nine were married or cohabiting, but 149 were single or separated in some way; thirty-nine were of no fixed abode; in 108 cases alcohol was involved at the time of offending; 156 were known to have previous convictions. Thus more were single than in the police sample (sixty-five per cent as against thirty-eight per cent), a similar percentage were of no fixed abode (nineteen per cent and seventeen per cent); alcohol was involved more frequently (forty-seven per cent and thirty-one per cent) and a greater proportion had previous convictions (sixty-eight per cent, and forty-nine per cent), in the procurator fiscal sample than in the police sample.

The difference in emphasis on the offence itself has been noted. A lengthy previous criminal record, particularly if it involved violence, was more likely to lead to medical referral by the procurator fiscal than by the police. For example:

Male, 20. Ten previous convictions including breach of the peace and police assault. Already in Borstal, Young Offenders' Institution and also in-patient hospital treatment. Charge: Breach of the peace and police assault. Previous in-patient treatment. 'An irresponsible and impulsive dullard who must learn to be responsible for the consequences of his own behaviour.' No medical recommendation.

Moreover in procurator fiscal cases as well as in those of the police, there was an indication of seeking help for social problems.

The psychiatric reports: place and time

Information was sought on the locus of the psychiatric examination and the time allowed for it. Some conflict of interest was apparent in relation to custody cases. Courts are reluctant to hold an accused in custody longer than necessary, and there is a need for a preliminary medical opinion within seven days where full committal is under consideration. This posed difficulties for psychiatrists. In thirty-seven cases it was noted that an interval of only seven days was allowed, but some procurators fiscal commented that just a brief report was required to allow a decision as to the next stage of court proceedings to be made; fourteen or twenty-one days' interval (sixty-four and forty-eight cases) was more usual.

A remand to hospital (instead of to prison) can only be made if a bed is available and this is basically a medical decision. Remands to prison not only increase the congestion in over-crowded accommodation for untried prisoners, but may also place an extra demand on prison staff if observation is needed for a mentally disturbed person. Ideally prison staff should be aware of those prisoners remanded for the purpose of psychiatric reports, but this is not always so and thus valuable information on observable behaviour, quoted as one advantage of custodial remand may be lost. If an accused is ordained to appear in court[12] then the psychiatrist is likely to be limited to one interview; time is lost if the appointment is not kept, and information from other sources on observed behaviour is not available unless a relative accompanies the patient. Against this must be set the great cost in resources, and in loss of liberty, by custodial remands—especially where a custodial sentence is not necessarily the ultimate disposal of the court.[13] There were some instances of persons originally remanded to prison who were thereafter transferred to hospital whilst still on remand. For example:

Male, 20, Charge: Indecent assault and breach of the peace. First examined in prison but remanded to hospital for the second psychiatric report. Found unfit to plead.

Female, 19, married. No previous convictions. Charge: Fire-raising. Started a fire in a hostel where she was working. Had been brought up in a children's home. Seen in legalised cells. Doctor unable to give opinion and she was transferred to a hospital for further assessment.

Most hospitals recognised the requirement to keep a remanded person in hospital until the next court appearance, even though not recommending any medical disposal. A problem arises in those cases where the seriousness of the offence or possible danger to the public outweigh medical considerations. There is a need for clarification between procurators fiscal and hospital staff on what is in fact understood by 'security' and indeed whether patients admitted from the courts are seen by hospitals as in need of, or are given, any security. One psychiatrist spoke of 'ground parole' while another spoke of a 'closed ward', but this refers to security in the hospital sense of preventing perhaps a confused patient from wandering; it is not security in the sense of preventing a determined person (and possibly a dangerous one) from leaving.[14]

Another doctor said it was made clear to the courts that the hospital was *not* a secure establishment, and that if a person was thought by the hospital staff to be too great a security risk, his removal to prison would be requested. Thus at present (again apart from one city with a secure forensic unit) it would seem that real security requires a custodial remand in prison or in a maximum security (special) hospital. Some issues of principle and practice arise for debate: for example, gravity of offence is equated with level of dangerousness by the court but this is not necessarily valid; the issue of how public risk or danger can be defined, how it can be recognised, and whose responsibility such recognition should be is unclear; once an accused is deemed violent or dangerous extra demands are made on prison resources.

The hospitals are able to select those whom they admit for observation or treatment; the prisons have no choice whatsoever, and, just as the police commented on responsibility and use of resources, so prison staff commented on those sent into their charge, whether on remand or sentenced, who they felt should be in hospital. What was referred to by one doctor as 'the asylum role of the prison' is an issue with many important implications. Prison staff see the prisons now being used to house and care for a substantial number of relatively harmless inadequates who, in previous years, might have been acceptable in mental hospitals. For example:

Male, 42, no fixed abode. 96 previous convictions. Current charge: theft when drunk. Known to mental hospital in 1966. Drinking except when in prison. No psychiatric recommendation. Outcome: 60 days' imprisonment.

Male, 49. Ten previous convictions including seven of fraud. Eight short-term imprisonments. Charge: Fraud. Two previous psychiatric reports indicated that he had been a patient since 1974, had been in and out of hospital, had had a severe head injury, and was a psychopathic personality. Psychiatric reports after examination in prison indicated no significant mental disorder and no psychiatric recommendation. Outcome: 9 months' sentence.

They were also able to identify a small but significant number of extremely violent offenders, many with a history of psychiatric treatment, who they felt would be more appropriately placed in a maximum security psychiatric hospital. For example:

A man who murdered a petrol pump attendant in the Borders was described as having a severe personality disorder, as being a psychopathic personality, a dangerous man, best dealt with in a prison with regular psychiatric contact, and he was an ex-inmate of a Special Prison. Another, who murdered a schoolgirl of 14 in hotel grounds was said to have marked psychopathic tendencies and he was a former patient of a State Hospital.

The place of the psychiatric examination in relation to the subsequent disposal for the procurator fiscal sample is shown in Table 4 and it can be seen that of the 123 people remanded to prison, forty-one or thirty-eight per cent did not receive custodial sentences. However, it must be remembered that time spent in prison on remand will be taken into consideration when sentence is passed by a sheriff.

TABLE 4

Scotland 1979: Sample of cases where psychiatric reports requested by procurator fiscal: disposal by place of psychiatric examination

Disposal	Place of psychiatric examination			Total	%
	Prison	Hospital	Other or not known		
No proceedings, admonition or discharge	13	12	2	27	12
Probation	17	22	3	42	19
Fine	11	14	4	29	12
Custodial	54	9	2	65	28
Sentence deferred	10	11	1	22	10
Hospital order	8	13		21	9
Other or not known	10	4	8	22	10
Total	123	85	20	228	
%	54	37	9		100

The routine for obtaining the mandatory second psychiatric report if a mental hospital disposal is recommended varies. In some areas the original request for a report includes a request to the first psychiatrist to obtain a second report: in others the procurator fiscal will request a second report direct from a named psychiatrist if the need seems likely; in other areas again there will be telephone communication between the first psychiatrist and the procurator fiscal, and the first psychiatrist will arrange to obtain the second report. Two reports are always obtained by the Crown in murder cases. In one city there are even three, there being also a report from the prison medical officer. Other than in murder cases, there were twenty-six instances of two reports being requested. Only two cases were noted of an independent defence report. The general procedure was for a defence lawyer to be given a copy, or be apprised of the contents, of the Crown psychiatric report. In one city, should the defence indicate a desire for a report, then it would be organised by the procurator fiscal, the rationale being that his office could arrange one more speedily and would in any case feel it desirable to obtain one if it was known that the defence wished it. One psychiatrist, routinely preparing court reports for the Crown, said he did not do defence work; others indicated their willingness to do such reports if asked. The rarity of conflicting opinions between prosecution and defence psychiatrists was noteworthy.

The psychiatric reports: results

The general complaint made by the courts related to the late arrival of reports—for example one procurator fiscal said a report tended to arrive *with* the prisoner for the court hearing, making any consideration of its contents, and instruction of deputes in advance, impossible. While a researcher was in his office this did happen: a case of rape where the report arrived *with* the accused in court and the depute procurator fiscal concerned had to seek an immediate adjournment to obtain instructions. On the other hand it was pointed out that the seven-day period available for some reports together with the delays in postal services made it impossible to guarantee that reports reached courts in time. The comment by one or two offices that reports contained pages of unnecessary detail, when all that was required was a conclusion and/or recommendation, stemmed from a lack of appreciation of the working methods of psychiatrists and the failure of procurators fiscal adequately to instruct psychiatrists.

It has been mentioned that no clear reason was given for requesting the psychiatric report in the majority of cases. Not surprisingly, few reports were therefore able to indicate the purpose of the examination, but most included a comment on the sources of information available to the reporting psychiatrist. This confirms the trend of seeking advice on those with previous problems—from 174 reports, 115 mentioned not only offence data but also previous medical or psychiatric information.

A simplified diagnostic analysis of sample cases is shown in Table 5:

TABLE 5

Scotland 1979: Procurator fiscal cases: diagnostic analysis

No mental disorder	50
Mental disorder	33
Personality disorder/psychopathy	41
Alcohol or drug abuse	39
Mental handicap	20
Epilepsy	1
Other	14
No clear medical statement available	30
	228

Misunderstandings between police and doctors arose principally over violent and troublesome offenders. Misunderstandings between procurators fiscal and doctors arose in similar circumstances—over the personality-disordered and even psychopathic offenders. Although 'psychopathic disorder' is not a term used in the Mental Health (Scotland) Act 1960, and although its medical definition is obscure, it continues to be used. Unrealistic expectations in some quarters that psychopathy is a definable medical condition, an illness amenable to treatment, lead to misunderstandings. There is confusion too even within the medical field. One psychiatrist commented that he equated treatment with cure and so did not admit psychopaths, but at the same time he felt that if such a person needed to be put outwith the community, then a hospital was more appropriate for this purpose than a prison.

A summary of psychiatric recommendations to procurators fiscal in relation to subsequent disposal of cases follows:

TABLE 6

Scotland 1979: Sample of cases where psychiatric reports requested by procurator fiscal: disposal by psychiatric recommendation

Disposal	No recommendation	Penal disposal	Probation or sentence deferred and treatment	Hospital in-patient	Other	Total	%
No proceedings, admonition or discharge	5	3	5	4	10	27	12
Probation	7	2	8		3	20	9
Probation with condition of treatment	1	1	11	1	8	22	10
Fine	11	10	2		6	29	12
Custodial	31	21	1		12	65	28
Sentence deferred	11	1	4		6	22	10
Hospital order				19	2	21	9
Other or not known	6	1	1		14	22	10
Total	72	39	32	24	61	228	
%	31	17	14	11	27		100

It is apparent that where specific psychiatric recommendations are made, and an indication is given of willingness to treat, or of a bed being available, then the court disposal is in line with this specialist advice. The court is unlikely to reject professional advice on the disposal of a case where that advice is within the provisions of legislation and is in accord with the climate of the court. The professionals, the psychiatrists, are able to select those whom they feel they can treat. The bulk of those referred are not offered treatment by the psychiatrists and a proportion of these cases will present severe and intractable problems to the sentencer as these examples show:

Male, 41, single. Over 30 previous convictions for breach of the peace and drunk and incapable. Fines and short prison sentences. History of psychiatric hospital. Charge: drunk and incapable. Personality disorder. Out-patient treatment offered but must be of his own volition. Social worker reports he cannot go back to hostel because of his drinking habits and that probation is not appropriate. Outcome: Fine £5.

Male, 21, single. Eight previous convictions for theft, drugs, road traffic offences. Currently on suspended sentence. Charge: assault and breach of the peace and taking and driving away under the influence of drugs. A known drug-user, recently released from a rehabilitation centre in England, already detained several times in mental hospital but always signs himself out. Police surgeon arranged admission to hospital on Section 31, but he discharged himself after 7 days. Outcome: 60 days' imprisonment.

Chapter 5

The Courts

This book is primarily concerned with problems of an offender's mental abnormality in the arrest and prosecution processes and clearly does not provide a forum for a detailed examination of sentencing issues. However it would seem illogical not to follow through from arrest and prosecution to disposal, if only because of the further opportunity provided in the court to seek psychiatric advice, after a finding or plea of guilt. The responsibility of directing a psychiatric examination within the criminal justice process before such a plea or finding lies with defence or prosecution: the judge's only opportunity of seeking it is in relation to sentencing. In practice such requests for reports in Scotland are often, for administrative convenience, channelled through procurator fiscal offices[1] and on that account have formed part of the research data.

The motive for deciding to seek medical advice is different in each service. The police seek advice on fitness to be detained, the procurators fiscal on fitness to be prosecuted, the sheriffs[2] on fitness to be sentenced. Both these latter court decisions come in the category of professional decision-making in criminal justice terms, but there are some differences between them. It could be argued that concepts of criminal justice govern conviction, but that an element of expediency or social responsibility is added to the concept of criminal justice when a sheriff considers sentencing. The procurator fiscal has to make an initial decision on reported information. The sheriff has reports, but by the time he has made up his mind to ask for a psychiatric report he has also seen the accused in court. Thus he has more information than has been available at either of the earlier decision points, and his is the last opportunity of seeking psychiatric advice. The decision he has to make can be fraught with serious consequences. The procurator fiscal service can identify cases omitted by the police, the sheriff can identify cases omitted by the procurators fiscal, but there is no check on cases missed by the sheriff; and while the discretion of police and fiscal has the effect of opening the gate into the criminal justice system, the decision-making role of the sheriff determines—to continue the metaphor—whether or not that gate shuts behind an offender as well as the manner and the length of stay behind it.

Information on the stage at which an accused's mental state is first called in question, and by whom, can only be given in very broad terms in this survey based on recorded information. In particular there is no indication of when, why and by whom *within* court proceedings the issue first came to be raised, apart from the broad division of plea and sentence.[3] It could be raised as the result of observed behaviour in court, of conversation formal or informal, of information from a witness or the defence lawyer, or it could originate in a sheriff's search for a guide to sentencing;[4] there are indeed some specific disposals which he could have in mind which are discussed later. The sheriff's decision to call for a psychiatric report is an individual one, perhaps more influenced by his personal views of its purpose and usefulness, than that of police or procurators fiscal. For instance a sheriff, known to be averse to locking anyone up, might see a report as a possible expedient to prevent it; even though such an attempt is not always successful.

> Male, married, 20. Four previous convictions. Charge: assault and breach of the peace. Assault and threats to his father when drunk. Psychiatric examination in prison. A substantial fine is recommended or 'a custodial sentence to dry him out'. Outcome: 60 days' imprisonment.

There were several instances where medical help or treatment had been offered but had failed or been rejected, and so responsibility for disposal returned to the courts.

> Male, 45, no fixed abode. Divorced. Twelve previous convictions. Charge: House-breaking and forgery to get money for alcohol. Psychiatric examination in prison. Long hospital involvement re alcoholism. Notable lack of motivation for treatment. 'He will be dried out in prison.' Social enquiry report: lacking motivation, probation to no advantage, request court to use some other method. Outcome: ten months' imprisonment.

> Male, 18, single. Nine previous convictions, mainly for offences after excessive drinking. Admonition, fined, detention centre and Borstal. Charge: violent and drunken behaviour in village street. History of hospital treatment for glue-sniffing. Psychiatric examination in prison. No mental illness. Sentence deferred for clinic help with glue-sniffing problem but did not keep appointment.

It was pointed out that different practices between areas could be the result of differing personal views rather than the result of inherent differences in offenders or exigencies of resources. Nevertheless there is some advantage to be gained by examining the routines, reasons and results of sheriffs' practices though our information is derived at second hand from court officials' interpretations both of the courts' proceedings and of the sheriffs' decision-making.

In general terms the court appeared to seek help in dealing with some form of social problem.

> Male, 20, single. Nine previous convictions (six of which for the theft of motor vehicles). Already admonition, fined, probation, Detention Centre, Borstal and Young Offenders' Institution. Charge: Take and drive away a motor vehicle. Reason for report: frequency of this offence and note of previous psychiatric advice after prolonged truanting from school. Psychiatric examination in prison. Personality disorder accompanied by depressive state. Need for in-patient treatment initially, but must return home for rehabilitation. Punishment has had no effect on his anti-social behaviour. Further offending before court disposal. Sentence deferred.

Male, 43. Seven previous convictions, breach of the peace, theft etc. Problem of alcohol. Charge: Breach of the peace. Psychiatric examination as hospital out-patient. Started drinking to excess because of domestic problems. Has made good progress with help to overcome addiction, agrees to attend at intervals as out-patient. Outcome: admonished.

The sentencer is seeking help with his task, but even with reports from all possible sources, such help may not be available. The ultimate and difficult responsibility is on the sheriff in court as the following case shows:

Female, 20, single. Previous convictions for breach of the peace and assault. Fine, admonition, hospital order and prison. Charge: assault and breach of the peace. Left the hostel where she was staying. Appeared to have epileptic fit in pub when drinking heavily. Admitted to hospital, struggling and fighting with staff. Psychiatric report in prison. Letter from governor 'On the advice of Crown Office and with the knowledge and support of the procurator fiscal, I wish to apply to the Sheriff dealing with the case for transfer to hospital. I foresee this girl shuttling in and out of prison until her mental state deteriorates sufficiently, or she offends sufficiently, to gain the necessary treatment but which by that time, can only be too late.' Two psychiatric reports from prison. Epileptic, history of overdoses, drinking, not psychotic or neurotic illness. 'Aggressive psychopathy because of her unpredictable violent behaviour towards patients and staff. We cannot offer to re-admit, nor is it likely that any other hospital can offer her a place. Because of the violent and impulsive nature of her behaviour, treatment under secure conditions would be necessary, and because of the relatively trivial nature of the offences, and the short sentences, together with pressure on accommodation, the State Hospital cannot offer to admit her either.' There is also a Social Enquiry report; 'Tragic and abhorrent as it may seem, it is not felt that the resources of this Department can be of any assistance to X' and reasons are given against probation. The outcome was a short Young Offenders' Institution sentence which in effect because of its back-dating, meant immediate release.

The psychiatric reports were obtained by the sheriff clerk direct or through procurator fiscal offices on lines already described, but the psychiatrist was rarely told why the report was wanted. In only fourteen out of 170 cases was there a clear request for a recommendation for disposal, and in only twelve psychiatric reports was such a request noted as the purpose of the report. Questions arise—why are reports requested? Who are the offenders concerned? Where do examinations take place? What advice is given? What decision is subsequently made?

Why? Who?

During a trial itself, mental disorder can only be considered in relation to fitness to plead or responsibility—either it amounts to a defence or it does not—and a psychiatrist may find himself giving evidence 'for' or 'against'. But mental disorder may become of importance again, and in a wider and somewhat different way, in relation to mitigation of sentence. In recent years the trend has been for many of the questions on mental disorder raised in court to be in relation to disposal.

With an awareness of this position, the reasons given for seeking a psychiatric report[5] in the sheriff courts in the Scottish sample were tabulated and set alongside the reasons for similar requests known to have been made by the prosecution, thus examining the two main stages of the court process.

TABLE 1

Scotland 1979: Recorded reasons for psychiatric reports in sheriff court sample and procurator fiscal sample (%)

	Sheriff court %	Procurator fiscal %
Nature of offence	36	35
Bizarre behaviour in relation to offending	3	13
History of psychiatric involvement or behaviour problems	26	20
Previous court order to hospital	3	2
Information from defence	4	2
Alcohol	21	12
Murder	—	16
Other	7	—
	100	100
	(n = 178)	(n = 166)

This table shows an emphasis on the nature of the offence and the past history of the offender at both stages. But as might have been expected, the element of bizarre behaviour figured more largely in relation to fitness to be prosecuted than did alcohol which is clearly seen as the greater problem in relation to sentencing. The inadequate petty recidivist with many social problems and a history of alcohol-related offending is an ever-recurring problem. The current consensus of opinion is that alcohol problems *per se* are not matters for the criminal courts, but neither are they always considered a medical responsibility.[6]

Male, 21. Fifteen previous convictions, breach of the peace, fraud, theft, misuse of drugs. Charge: Uttering. Obtaining drugs on forged prescription form. Psychiatric examination as hospital out patient. Sane and fit to plead. Has been heavy drinker and dependent on drugs. Claims to have given both up and does not wish psychiatric treatment. Disposal by court recommended without regard to his past history. Outcome: fine £50 or sixty days.

Male, 32, separated. One previous conviction, drunk and incapable. Charge: Breach of the peace (drunk and aggressive). A record of nine hospital in-patient periods for overdoses, wrist slashing, bouts of heavy drinking. Psychiatric examination in prison. Has had a great deal of help and treatment from many hospitals. Frequent suicidal gestures. A far-gone alcoholic. Psychiatric treatment has failed, but an informal relationship with out-patient clinic can help. The court should impose whatever penalties appropriate. Outcome: Sentence deferred to be of good behaviour.

Requests for reports may indicate that a judge is seeking information as to the extent of an offender's social responsibility, even though his criminal responsibility has been decided. It may also indicate in the judge's own considerations a sense of social responsibility to others, but can also show a judge's own perplexity over the suitability of sentences: property offences and breaches of the peace figure prominently in requests for reports, although sentencing here may follow a routine.

Male, 18. Previous convictions for housebreaking and theft. Charge: Eight housebreakings plus absconding from hospital when on remand. Psychiatric examinations: one in prison then transferred to hospital for assessment. Recommendation made for probation with condition of treatment, but behaviour in hospital deteriorated, and he absconded. Further reports from procurator fiscal. Psychiatric examination in prison. Report refers to effort made in hospital when he absconded, and had no intention of co-operating. Impulsive, irresponsible. Sane and fit to plead. No medical recommendation and law should take its course. Outcome: fine £250.

Male, 21, no fixed abode, unemployed, single. Twelve previous convictions, breach of the peace, theft, road traffic offences. Probation, fine, Borstal, Young Offenders' Institution, imprisonment. Currently released on Young Offender's licence. Charge: housebreaking and theft of cars. Psychiatric examination in prison. Severe personality disorder with psychopathic features. Not motivated to treatment. Past attempts to treat have failed. Attempt to treat a waste of professional time. Law should take its normal course. Social Enquiry Report refers to no respect for law, social work nothing to offer, open to any disposal which the court feels is appropriate. Outcome: Nine months' imprisonment.

The frequency with which reports are obtained in cases of sexual offences suggests that judges are aware of public anxiety and the need to prevent repeated offending. They may however be unaware of the therapeutic pessimism in contemporary psychiatry in relation to successful treatment for sex offenders and the problems of treating such individuals within the legal constraints imposed by a sentence.

Male, 22, single, unemployed. One previous conviction, lewd and libidinous practices, hospital order. Charge: lewd and libidinous practices. Psychiatric examination in prison. Previously in mental handicap hospital. Limited intellectual capacity. Emotionally immature. High grade mental defective. No evidence of violence or aggressive sexual behaviour. Perhaps long-term probation. Second psychiatric report. Passive, gentle, nuisance to community because of impulsive sexual behaviour to young children. Does not require medical or nursing care. Suggest probation. 'A responsible social worker will have to take total commitment for care, control and guidance for this person.' Social Work Enquiry Report also referred to mental defect, a supportive home, immature sexually, but no violence or aggression and suggested social work advice to parents and help to the man through probation. Outcome: Probation, three years.

Male, 30, single, employed. Numerous charges of breach of the peace and lewd and libidinous practices. No previous convictions. Psychiatric examination at his own home. No evidence of psychiatric disorder or deviant sexual orientation. He denies charges and due process of law should operate. Outcome: Charges proven, fine £150.

Demographic data stress the multiple social problems of offenders where reports are sought. In the Scottish sample of 184, with a sex ratio of three males to one female, seventy-four per cent were single or separated in some way and thirteen per cent were of no fixed abode, while only twenty-two per cent were known to be married or cohabiting. In forty-three per cent of cases alcohol was involved at the time of offending. Sixty-eight per cent had previous convictions, with sixteen per cent having eleven or more. Forty-nine per cent had some previous record of breach of the peace or assault. This information underlines the problems presented by the petty recidivist.

Female, 40, married. Nine previous convictions, theft, etc. Probation, admonition, fine and prison. Charge: Theft (two). Shoplifting on two consecutive days at same shop, and oddness about articles stolen and the repetition of the offence. Psychiatric examination as hospital out-patient. An inadequate personality and distress of debts resulting in unhappy, confused state of mind. Neither custodial nor monetary penalty appropriate. Outcome: one year probation.

Male, 52, unemployed, single. Ten previous convictions, breach of the peace, etc. Current charge: Indecent assault after drinking. Psychiatric examination in prison. No mental illness. Family pattern of drinking. Prognosis poor, medical intervention no part to play in his management. No suggestion to make. Previously admitted to hospital on three occasions, but twice discharged because returned intoxicated. Social Enquiry Report: 'His aim each day is to obtain and consume as much alcohol as possible. Suggest disposal for psychiatric treatment.' Outcome: sixty days imprisonment.

There is a marked similarity in this information, summarised from Scottish survey data in 1979, to a list of suggested categories of offenders where psychiatric advice might usefully be sought presented by Nigel Walker in *Sentencing in a Rational Society*:[7]

    (i)   the mature person who, after years of steady, respectable living, is unexpectedly detected in some 'out of character' offence, such as embezzlement or assault; and, as an extreme case, any first offender over sixty years of age;

   (ii)   at the other extreme, the offender with a history of persistent anti-social behaviour which fails to respond to ordinary correctives;

  (iii)   the offender whose offences have an irrational quality about them, especially if they follow a stereotyped pattern (for example, the man who picks up and then assaults prostitutes, or steals only women's clothing);

  (iv)   the offender who commits serious violence against members of his own family;

   (v)   most sexual offenders, apart from those who have simply had intercourse with willing girls just under the age of consent.

Where?

The location of the psychiatric assessment is important particularly if the request means a period in prison or in hospital for an offender who may not subsequently receive a custodial sentence. In the Scottish sample sixty per cent of cases were deferred for twenty-one days for reports; nevertheless one sheriff commented on the fact that the report was only available with his papers in *court* resulting in time-wasting delay while he read it. Furthermore both the discussion of contents and their further elucidation were discouraged, and, as a result less time could be available for decision-making. Reports received in advance were seen as more valuable and more effective.

Under section 54 of the Mental Health (Scotland) Act 1960 the sheriff courts in Scotland can remand an offender directly to hospital for psychiatric examination, a facility not available in the English courts at the time of the research, but now possible under section 35 of the Mental Health Act 1983. Five cases in the sample were dealt with in this way. Also Scottish courts appear to use the power to ordain an offender to appear for a psychiatric examination as an out-patient more than do English courts,[8] and also to use this power more in relation to sentencing than to prosecution—forty-five per cent as against twenty-two per cent. This difference is an understandable one, because critical issues of sanity and fitness to plead, as well as immediate issues of violence or danger which necessitate custody, should have been resolved earlier in the criminal justice process. Nevertheless, half the offenders were still remanded to prison for examination, but it must be acknowledged that the question of hospital security arises. This issue is discussed in detail elsewhere (references in Chapters 4, 6 and 7), but there are growing signs of the awareness of the courts that 'secure' may mean different things in medical and criminal justice terms. This is especially so in Scotland, since the *Harkins* case. (For discussion see

Chapter 7.) Not only are courts more aware of the limitations of hospital security, but hospitals are more reluctant to accept the offender who may present a serious security risk. The place of remand in relation to disposals within the criminal justice system is shown in Table 2:

TABLE 2

Scotland 1979: Sample of cases where psychiatric reports requested by sheriff court: disposal by place of psychiatric examination

Disposal	Place of psychiatric examination				Total	%
	Prison	Hospital in-patient	Hospital out-patient or clinic	Other or not known		
Admonition or discharge	11		11		22	12
Probation	14		17	2	33	18
Probation with condition of treatment	9	1	23	1	34	18
Fine	9		16		25	14
Custodial	34		3	1	38	21
Sentence deferred	10	2	7		19	10
Hospital order	3		2		5	3
Other or not known	2		3	3	8	4
Total	92	3	82	7	184	
%	50%	1%	45%	4%		100%

The fact that eighty-two per cent of those ordained to appear as out-patients were subsequently given non-custodial disposals in the form of probation or fines should come as no surprise and it can be surmised that medical advice confirmed sentencers' own views and inclinations.

Male, 37, married. No previous convictions. Charge: lewd and libidinous practices after drinking. History of hospital admission for depression. Psychiatric examination as out-patient. Incident completely out of character: isolated and unpremeditated due to excessive drinking. No treatment called for. Prison would be harmful. Outcome: probation.

Male, 61, employed, home, married. No previous convictions. Charge: Breach of the peace. Dressed in female clothes, exposed underwear to pedestrian. Seen as out-patient. Report said badly shaken by car accident. Similar dressing up episode twenty years previously. No mental illness. Suggest lenient disposal and monetary penalty. Fined—amount unknown.

Male, 48, divorced. No previous convictions. Charge: Breach of the peace, disorderly and noisy behaviour in the street. Psychiatric examination as out-patient. Admission to psychiatric hospitals and out-patient treatment over the years. Suffering from mental illness but sane and fit to plead. Has failed in the past to comply with requirements for treatment. Probation order recommended to ensure his attendance. Treatment is essential. Sentence deferred to attend hospital and accept treatment as advised.

What may cause concern, however, is the fact that while thirty-four of the ninety-two (thirty-seven per cent) remanded in custody for psychiatric reports were subsequently given custodial sentences, there were fifty-three cases (fifty-eight per cent) who, after spending time on remand, were given non-custodial disposals.

Male, 23, single. Twenty previous convictions including fifteen breach of the peace. Probation, admonition, fines and prison. Charge: Breach of the peace, disturbance in father's home after drinking, threatened mother with poker. History of epilepsy and drinking and psychiatric attention. Psychiatric examination in prison; suffering from anti-social personality disorder. Psychiatric treatment not recommended, epilepsy well under control. Outcome: fine £150.

Male, 22, single. Two previous convictions, breach of the peace and assault. Charge: Breach of the peace. Ejected from a house because of drunkenness. Went back and created disturbance. Psychiatric report in prison. Admits to excessive drinking. No mental illness. Recommend deferred sentence with condition to attend alcoholics' clinic. Outcome: Deferred sentence as recommended.

There is no way of knowing whether the time already spent in custody was taken into account in individual cases by individual sentencers, but it should also be remembered that remand prisoners as a whole form about fifteen per cent[9] of the average daily population in Scottish prisons, and that custodial remand followed by non-custodial disposal is not confined to those with suspected mental disorders.

What are the special powers of sentencers in relation to the mentally disturbed, and what advice did they receive to aid them towards the disposals in Table 2.

The sheriff, having received psychiatric advice, and normally also a Social Enquiry Report, indicating some need for consideration of mental disorder has additional sentencing options open to him, save where the penalty is one fixed by law. In any case where imprisonment would be a competent disposal he may impose a hospital order where the broad aspects of the case include issues of public concern, an element of society's responsibility for the offender; but because the effect of a hospital order is to transfer decision-making power from the legal to the medical field where release is concerned, there is a counter balance in the interests of public safety. The courts have the right, when they feel protection may be required from an offender whose history is such that he may re-offend *as a result of his mental disorder* if released, to make an order restricting discharge for a specified period or without limit of time. This requires oral evidence from an approved medical practitioner, and has the effect of vesting all control of transfer or release of the offender in the hands of the Secretary of State.

Provisions, similar in principle though with minor differences in operation, are available in England and Wales (*see* Appendix 1). It was in a discussion of the English situation that Walker[10] pointed out that there need be no connection between the offence and the mental disorder to justify a hospital order. Indeed he has written of the restriction order as being 'designed to protect the public against the over-optimism or irresponsibility of psychiatrists' in releasing from mental hospitals. He refers to such orders as 'a warning but not an injunction' where society is concerned, pointing out that the 'restriction order does not guarantee secure custody for it does not oblige an ordinary hospital to impose *any* physical restraint on the offender-patient'.

Among further possible medical disposals are deferred sentences or probation orders with a requirement of psychiatric treatment up to a period of one year, although the probation order itself has a possible three-year maximum. The problem inherent in the probation order arises here because the offender must be willing to accept probation, and should he cease to accept the psychiatric treatment involved (and if the probation officer is so advised by the medical authorities) the only recourse of the probation officer is re-referral to the courts.

Female, 21, single, unemployed. Thirteen previous convictions for breach of the peace, assault, theft, etc. Fines, Borstal, probation, and Young Offenders' Institution. Charge: Shoplifting and malicious damage. Shoplifting in supermarket, damage to mattress in police cell when arrested, under tranquillisers and alcohol at the time. History of psychiatric hospital involvement. Psychiatric report—hospital. Referred to seven previous admissions in the past two years. Serious drinking problem. Aggressive and violent when apprehended. Suicide attempts. A personality disorder characterised by immature and irresponsible behaviour. Second report: behaves impulsively and self-destructively, then follows institutional care in either hospital or prison. Danger of becoming dependent on such care. Essential she is given help to deal with difficulties in the community. Probation and out-patient treatment recommended. Outcome: two-year probation with condition of clinic attendance.

Male, 17, single. No previous convictions. Culpable fire-raising, and malicious damage. Psychiatric examination in prison. Has a lot of psychiatric problems. Needs help. Suggest probation and treatment. Outcome: two years' probation with one year out-patient treatment.

Again to quote Walker,[11] 'It would be very difficult to argue that there is any rational and objective distinction between offences by disordered persons which lead to disposal by a court and those which are dealt with in one of the unofficial ways . . . given that the perpetrator has acquired the official status of patient or ex-patient, quite serious incidents may be handled unofficially, just as quite trivial ones may lead to hospital orders.'

Male, 18, single. Five previous convictions including road traffic, lewd and libidinous practices and theft. Fine, probation and List D School. Previous psychiatric treatment. Charge: lewd and libidinous practices. Psychiatric report in prison. Had treatment earlier, but terminated when the accused did not keep appointments. Court should deal with him without taking account of his mental state. Outcome: Borstal.

Male, 37, married. No previous convictions. Charge: lewd and libidinous practices after drinking. History of hospital admission for depression. Psychiatric examination as out-patient. Incident completely out of character. Isolated and unpremeditated due to excessive drinking. No treatment called for. Prison would be harmful. Outcome: Probation.

This question of a psychiatric history being known and the possible 'official status of patient or ex-patient' is clearly important. From 170 reports examined, 145 (eighty-five per cent) referred to medical information being known or available.

What advice did these psychiatric reports give?

The advice to the court is summarised in Table 3, with a note of similar advice given to procurators fiscal (i.e. at the earlier stage of criminal proceedings) alongside for comparison:

TABLE 3

Scotland 1979: Psychiatric advice to sheriff court and procurator fiscal where known

	Sheriff clerk		Procurator fiscal	
	No.	%	No.	%
Sane and fit to plead (court disposal assumed)	66	36	129	57
Court disposal with treatment	35	19	11	5
Court disposal clearly stated	31	17	21	9
Illness (not in terms of Act)—treat	10	5	6	3
Mentally ill—hospital necessary	6	3	15	7
Insane at time of offence: now sane	1	1	2	1
Other	25	14	8	3
Not known	10	5	36	16
	184	100	228	100

A simple medical analysis of the information contained in these reports was made by a psychiatrist and this is summarised in Table 4:

TABLE 4

Scotland 1979: Medical analysis of information in psychiatric reports to sheriff court

	Sheriff clerk		Procurator fiscal	
	No.	%	No.	%
'No mental disorder'	48	26	50	22
'Mental disorder'	18	10	33	14
Personality disorder/psychopath	34	18	41	18
Alcohol or drug abuse	44	24	39	17
Mental handicap	14	8	20	9
Epilepsy	2	1	1	
Other/Not available	24	13	44	20
	184	100	228	100

Differences between the two groups reflect the difference in the decision-making roles of fiscal and sheriff. Problems of mental illness or of mental handicap appear in relation to prosecution, whereas recommendations for court disposals and diagnosis of alcohol abuse reflect the desire for guidance in sentencing.

What use did the sheriffs make of the advice given?

A summary of specific psychiatric recommendations to sheriff courts in relation to the criminal justice disposals made by the sheriffs concerned is given in Table 5.

Thus in almost half the cases a disposal of sentence deferred (ten per cent) or probation in some form (thirty-six per cent) was made, a significant increase from the approximate one per cent of cases dealt with by probation in total court disposals.[12] The singling out of some offenders as possibly in need of psychiatric treatment clearly has an effect.

When medical disposals were examined it was found, as expected, that in the five cases in the survey when a hospital order was advised this was put into effect. It is apparent that, as with the sample of procurator fiscal cases, where specific psychiatric recommendations are made, and an indication is given of willingness to treat or of a bed being available, the court disposal is in line with this specialist advice. As one would expect, the court is unlikely to reject professional advice on the disposal of a problem case where the acceptance of that advice is within the provisions of legislation. It may be that there is a conflict of advice—a professional social work recommendation being rejected by the psychiatrist.

TABLE 5

Scotland 1979: Sample of cases where psychiatric reports requested by sheriff court: disposal by psychiatric recommendation

| | Psychiatric recommendation | | | | | | |
Disposal	No recommendation	Penal disposal	Probation or sentence deferred and treatment	Hospital in-patient	Other	Total	%
Admonition or discharge	9	3	7		3	22	12
Probation	15	6	10		2	33	18
Probation with condition of treatment	3	1	28		2	34	18
Fine	15	7	3			25	14
Custodial	21	11	2	3	1	38	21
Sentence deferred	4	5	7	1	2	19	10
Hospital order				5		5	3
Other or not known	2	1	2		3	8	4
Total	69	34	59	9	13	184	
%	38%	18%	32%	5%	7%		100%

Female, 21. Previous convictions not known. Charge: Breach of the peace. She had attempted suicide, been in hospital and discharged, would not stay in her hostel, was arrested in the end by long-suffering police. Psychiatric examination in prison. Of dull/normal intelligence. Attention-seeking. Childish speech simulated. A term of control under a probation order suggested. No sign of mental illness, hospital admission not recommended. Social Enquiry Report said severely mentally disturbed and fulfill criteria for compulsory admission under Section 24. 'Committal to secure psychiatric hospital is necessary.' Outcome: Three years' probation.

The professionals, the psychiatrists, are able to select those whom they feel they can treat. The remaining problem cases are returned to the courts.

The number of cases where there may be an element of mental abnormality is few in relation to the totality of offenders. With procurators fiscal and sheriffs, as with the police, there is evidence of the seeking of a gateway to find help in solving social problems. Serious crimes are few indeed but, perhaps because of their rarity, there may be a lack of appreciation of the consequences of the decisions made. For example, acquittal on the grounds of insanity at the time of the offence does not always *have* to result in a State Hospital disposal if there are good reasons for containment in a normal mental hospital.[13] A further example is found in an appeal decision which quashed a four-year prison sentence for culpable homicide and instead substituted a deferred sentence for one year to allow treatment. The woman, who had turned to drink and drugs after the breakdown of her marriage, had subsequently become emotionally dependent on her aged mother to the extent that, rather than have her mother admitted to hospital, her pathological attachment led her to inflict injuries on her mother from which she died. A prison sentence, it was stated, had to be considered against the background of the circumstances of the case and the medical advice, and in the light of that advice this sentence could not stand; moreover there were other and better ways of dealing with the problem, it was reported. In another case there was evidence of compassionate interpretation and understanding concerning a woman facing a murder charge who was released from prison on bail after psychiatric reports; the charge was reduced to culpable homicide and the ultimate disposal one of probation with medical treatment. (There were seventeen cases noted where there was a reduction of charge which appeared to be related to the psychiatric reports.)

The sample of requests for psychiatric reports from sheriff clerks has shown a pattern similar to that in requests from procurators fiscal. What it is important to remember is that the final disposal of the offenders for whom reports are sought in each group of cases lies with the sheriff. The information available at point of sentence is much fuller than at the earlier stages in the criminal justice process. The documents will often include Social Enquiry Reports (which are not examined in detail in this project), which may give a wealth of background information, while the sheriff has the opportunity personally to observe the offender in court. The sheriff thus makes his decision on an offender, combining the advantages of both the police in knowing 'what he is' and the procurator fiscal in knowing 'what he has done': which thus combines and confirms the decisions taken at the earlier stages. At the same time it may be a decision combining elements of criminal justice and of expediency[14] in the wide range of non-penal disposals which are available after conviction.

Serious questions currently require further discussion. Does the existence of mental abnormality entitle the offender to greater consideration than is given to the normal offender, since this is what would appear to happen? Does the existence of mental abnormality entitle the public to greater protection than from the normal criminal? For this is how it appears from the terms of a restriction order. Should the medical profession select those few that it can treat in terms of its current thinking and remove them from the criminal justice system, leaving others to be dealt with by courts and prisons? For this again would appear to be the current position. Should consideration then be given to this vicarious responsibility placed on police, courts and prisons and to the resources that they should additionally be given to enable them to deal humanely and efficiently with the many offenders possibly suffering from a mental disorder who are left in their care?

Chapter 6

The Medical View

The great majority of offenders pass through the criminal courts without any reference being made to their mental condition, and the degree of overlap between the criminal justice and mental health care systems represents a tiny fraction of the total workload in each of these organisations. The extent of this area of overlapping interests can be examined in two ways.

Firstly, the criminal statistics for Scotland in 1978, for example, reveal that 146,945 persons were proceeded against for offences other than those involving motor vehicles. In the same year, 123 people were admitted to hospitals under Part V of the Mental Health (Scotland) Act 1960. Thus 1 in 1200 or 0.05 per cent of offenders were suffering from a mental disorder of such a serious nature that it required compulsory hospital admission. A certain number of offenders would have been dealt with by way of a probation order with a condition of psychiatric treatment, but their number would not make a serious impact on those quoted. A larger number of accused or convicted people would have been psychiatrically assessed at some stage during the judicial proceedings and some of these would, of course, have been found to suffer from a degree of mental disorder falling short of that which is required for compulsory admission.

Considered against the background of the total population of offenders, the seriously mentally disordered representing less than 0.1 per cent constitute an extremely small proportion. Although this small proportion may cause problems beyond any assessment based on their number, the temptation to regard all problem cases as mentally disordered (and then to cite the mental disorder as the reason for the problem) must be resisted. It is an example of the circular thinking which confounds much of the discussion on the complex relationship between crime and mental disorder.

A second way of looking at the numbers involved is to consider offender patients against the background of the total number of patients admitted to psychiatric hospitals. In 1979 there were 26,429 such admissions in Scotland. Nearly sixty per cent of these were admitted directly from general practitioners or from psychiatric out-patient clinics. In comparison only 2.5 per cent were admitted from a prison or from a judicial source of referral such as a criminal court. From the point of view of the hospital the 'forensic' source of admissions is extremely small and any special needs which this group have must be considered against the overall requirement of resources for the patient population as a whole.

Offender patients do not have any special needs simply because they are offenders. In common with other individuals suffering from some form of mental disorder their medical needs will be dependent upon the nature and severity of their condition. When discussing mentally abnormal offenders there is an unfortunate tendency to think in terms of locked doors and high walls, and inadequate consideration is given to the range of treatment facilities that are required. People suffering from psychiatric illnesses, be they offenders or not, require treatment facilities which are appropriate for their particular condition. Even during the course of one person's illness the clinical requirements may vary as improvement takes place. Thus high levels of staff supervision, and some degree of physical security, for example a locked door, may at some stage be necessary in order to provide optimal nursing care while avoiding the likelihood of self-injury or perhaps injury to others. The important point is that treatment requirements depend on the illness and not simply on whether or not the patient is an offender.

Changing trends in psychiatric care

There is little doubt that the style and method of functioning of psychiatric hospitals has changed considerably in the last two decades. Although voluntary treatment had been available prior to 1959 the Mental Health Act of the same year facilitated and encouraged this form of admission. For many years now less than ten per cent of psychiatric hospital patients are detained on a compulsory basis. There is less emphasis on practice which might be considered purely paternalistic or custodial and psychiatric hospitals have tried to meet the expectation of an increasingly well-informed consumer society. With all admissions the primary aim is to treat the patient and return him or her to the community, so that approximately seventy per cent of patients now admitted to psychiatric hospitals are discharged by the end of one month. Parallel with these developments has come the expansion of community-based resources so that a great deal of treatment is provided on an out-patient basis or in day centres.

Some would say that the modern emphasis on treatability and rapid discharge has become a preoccupation. Together with this there has been a reduction in the provision of locked wards in psychiatric hospitals and an increasing reluctance to provide asylum for a range of individuals who, for want of a better term, can only be described as 'socially inadequate'. It has been said that the pendulum has swung too far, and that psychiatric hospitals have become excessively selective concerning their admissions to the point where they no longer provide a reasonable service to the community. Whatever view is taken there will be no turning back the clock; it is not possible for psychiatric hospitals to revert to their former role. Thus they do not exist simply to provide board and lodging to the destitute and indeed, if that is the essential requirement there are much less costly alternatives available. Moreover Government policy, particularly in England but less so in Scotland, has directed resources away from long-stay hospital provision for the mentally ill and mentally handicapped. Residential facilities in the community, however, have not developed to the extent that was envisaged with the result that many mentally disabled individuals, usually harmless but often vulnerable, remain rootless and unsupported in society. The high incidence of mental disorders of varying degrees among vagrants and doss-house residents has been well described; many of these folk have substantial histories of psychiatric hospital care. It is not surprising that long-stay hospital facilities tend to be reserved for those cases that are seen as having the greatest clinical need. It might well be that the assessment of this 'need' is adjudged differently by the staff of mental hospitals than it would be by the staff of other agencies.

What needs to be emphasised however are some of the positive benefits that have accrued from these changes. The most important among these is that admission to a psychiatric hospital has lost a little of its former stigma. This encourages people to seek early treatment for their psychological difficulties without the fear that they will be incarcerated in a forbidding institution. The improved environment within the hospitals is reflected in a relaxed atmosphere without the oppressive levels of security which were formerly a feature. Psychiatrists and psychiatric nurses gain job-satisfaction from seeing themselves as therapists, rather than custodians, and there has been a massive expansion in the ancillary disciplines of clinical psychology and occupational therapy.

These developments have taken place at a price; in addition to the mounting hospital rejection of the 'inadequate' group, offender-patients have found that they too are often less than welcome in the modern psychiatric hospital. In the last decade there has been a drastic fall in the numbers of such patients accepted by hospitals for treatment from the courts. While a lack of suitable facilities is an argument frequently advanced for their rejection, many of these individuals require no special facilities beyond those already provided in most psychiatric hospitals. What then is the real reason for their rejection? This question was one of many considered in a recent report by the Royal College of Psychiatrists (1980).[1] The Report did not identify any single, outstanding reason but it drew attention to a number of attitudes and perceptions which seemed to underlie the difficulties.

The open-door policy in modern psychiatric units has been warmly welcomed by hospital staff, who fear that any moves to increase the numbers of offender patients being admitted will inevitably hinder this policy, and result in a return to more locked wards and other security measures. Coupled with this attitude is the desire by psychiatric hospital staff to see themselves as 'treaters' and not 'jailers'. The Royal College of Psychiatrists' Report noted that hospital staff, as a result of these attitudes, have become increasingly intolerant of violent behaviour by patients, to the extent that they become unwilling to accept that such violence can result from the patient's illness. Thus violence, whatever the cause, comes to be seen as a matter for the penal rather than the medical services, even in cases where there is clear evidence of severe mental illness. It is thus easy to see that staff have become less experienced in coping with violent behaviour and less tolerant of it. Anxiety by nurses concerning their own legal situation, when they have to restrain disturbed patients, is yet another ingredient adding to the overall unease. Nursing unions have been active in their efforts to secure the physical welfare and the legal rights of their members, and the Department of Health and Social Security recognises, by way of a pay lead, the special nature of the work in those units which are designated as a secure facility.

Certain matters relating to policy were also felt by the College to be important. For example, the building fabric and the physical structure of psychiatric units in many District General Hospital Units rendered them ill-equipped to manage patients requiring any degree of security. A recommendation by the Confederation of Health Service Employees (and one incidentally accepted by the Royal College of Psychiatrists), that a ward, or room, should be set aside in all psychiatric units to cater for disturbed patients, remains a counsel of perfection which is frequently unattainable.

Psychiatric treatment and offender-patients

To say that the purpose of psychiatric treatment is to cure the patient of his illness is a gross over-simplification and the aims of psychiatric treatment in general warrant some examination. The situation is comparable with medical disorders as a whole. Thus some conditions can be cured, some can be modified or controlled whilst not being eliminated, and for others treatment has little or nothing to offer. Finally, for those individuals who do not suffer from any form of psychiatric disorder there can be no expectation of a psychiatric remedy. This last statement may state the obvious but in fact today a large proportion of individuals referred to psychiatric clinics do not suffer from any form of mental illness in the formal sense of that term. In the current research the psychiatric conditions which were most frequently evident fell into four main groups:

1 patients with acute psychotic illnesses. That is to say a florid illness manifested by gross disturbances of thinking, perception, mood and behaviour in which the individual appeared totally out of touch with reality. Such conditions approximate to the legal concept of insanity;
2 individuals with abnormal personalities ranging from the periodically unstable to the severely antisocial. This latter group attract the psychiatric and legal term 'psychopathic disorder';
3 those whose predominant problem is one of alcohol or drug abuse. In this group there may sometimes, but by no means always, be an associated abnormality of personality, and even more rarely there may be an associated mental illness perhaps of a psychotic type;
4 a miscellaneous group showing some, or all of the following features:
   —no signs of florid mental illness but a previous history of perhaps quite lengthy hospital care;
   —homelessness;
   —periodic alcohol abuse;
   —a borderline degree of mental handicap.

For want of a better term this group is usually given the blanket description 'socially inadequate'.

Let us first examine these four groups in terms of their requirement for, and likely benefit from, medical treatment, and then see to what extent their status as offenders alters the situation.

1   Offenders with psychotic illnesses

All psychiatrists (with perhaps a few exceptions across the Atlantic) would agree that patients in this group must receive psychiatric treatment. If this is not possible on an informal or voluntary basis than it is quite likely to be undertaken using the compulsory civil powers of the Mental Health Acts. They will certainly benefit from treatment which might provide anything from total cure to temporary amelioration. Whatever the efficacy of the treatment may be, these people are accepted as a medical responsibility, and whether they have committed murder or a breach of the peace (and the second is more likely than the first) they are almost bound to receive a psychiatric disposal in court. Few would suggest that prison is an appropriate place for an offender suffering from a psychotic illness, yet attention has been drawn by the Director of the Prison Medical Service to the large number of just such people currently in that situation (Orr, 1978).[2] In Scotland, for a variety of reasons, the problem does not seem as great but inevitably prison remand wings are bound to contain such individuals. If clinical need alone was the determinant of psychiatric hospital admission then such people would not be in prison. Unfortunately, for reasons previously discussed, this is not the case, so that offender patients suffering from psychotic illnesses received less satisfactory care than their similarly afflicted non-offender counterparts.

2   Psychopathic offenders

With psychotic offenders there is at least some agreement on what the ideal situation should be; everyone accepts that they should be in hospital not prison. In relation to the second category of offenders, the personality-disordered, and in particular the psychopaths, there is fierce controversy and disagreement not only between, but also within, the professions. Once again let us first examine the psychiatric need for treatment and then turn to offender aspects. A large number of patients whose major psychiatric problem is an abnormality of personality are admitted to psychiatric hospitals each year and an even greater number are seen as out-patients. The great majority of such patients who are admitted receive treatment on an informal basis and the time spent in hospital is unlikely to be in excess of two weeks and may well be nearer two days. If compulsory powers are utilised they will be of the emergency type authorising detention for seventy-two hours only. These practices reflect the fact that, as far as the treatment of most personality disorders is concerned, the psychiatric cupboard is pretty bare. Psychiatric admission will be used to defuse a transient crisis situation and for this limited purpose it is useful.

A legacy of post-war psychiatric optimism, together with an insatiable consumer demand for medical resources, means that many people with personality disorders are referred, but in practice only a very few are treated by admission to hospital. A small number of specialised psychiatric units (for example, the Henderson Hospital in Surrey—recently under threat of closure) cater specifically for personality-disordered patients but invariably such patients can only be treated on a voluntary basis. Occupying a position at the extreme end of the spectrum of personality disorders is that condition, known as psychopathic disorder, and defined in Section 1 of the Mental Health Act 1983 as 'a persistent disorder or disability of mind (whether or not including subnormality of intelligence) which results in abnormally aggressive or seriously irresponsible conduct on the part of the patient, and requires or is susceptible to medical treatment'. This category of mental disorder, and in particular its medical and legal status, has been a source of lengthy debate and public concern. Society, through its philosophers, jurists and more recently through its social scientists, has always recognised that some individuals behave in a persistently and grossly anti-social manner and that these individuals seem unaffected by any punishment the courts care to impose. The name that has been given to this group of offenders has changed over the years in accordance with prevailing social attitudes and beliefs. During the last century, and the early decades of this one, the defect was thought to reside in the moral sense. Thus the terms 'moral insanity' and later 'moral defective' were adopted. The development of psycho-analytical theory in the inter-war years, followed by the medical advances of the 1950s, engendered a strongly medical view of the psychopath which was persuasively argued by influential psychiatrists of the day such as Sir David Henderson in Edinburgh and Edward Glover in London. In 1957 the Royal Commission on Mental Illness and Mental Deficiency,[3] impressed by the medical evidence, recommended that psychopathic disorder be recognised in law as a category of mental disorder and exactly just that followed in the Mental Health Act 1959 for England and Wales and subsequently the Mental Health Act 1983. The Scottish Mental Health Act, whilst avoiding the term 'psychopathic disorder', employs a descriptive phrase which embraces exactly the same psychiatric category, so that for practical purposes the law, north and south of the Border, is identical.

Although the courts are empowered to commit psychopaths to hospital, very few such offenders in this survey received hospital disposals. Indeed an almost universal view expressed by psychiatrists to the researchers was that this form of mental disorder could no longer be considered amenable to psychiatric treatment. Perhaps the most authoritative endorsement of this opinion came from the Butler Committee who stated: 'the great weight of evidence presented to us tends to support the conclusion that psychopaths are not, in general, treatable, at least in medical terms'. The Government,

having toyed with the idea of eliminating the category of psychopathic
disorder from the Mental Health Act, eventually decided to retain it
(Department of Health and Social Security, Home Office, Welsh Office,
Lord Chancellor's Department: 1981),[4] whilst at the same time adding a
'prospect of benefit from treatment' rider (section 3, Mental Health Act,
1983). In those instances where psychopaths are ordered to hospital by the
court, the destination will almost certainly be a special hospital of
maximum security. In Scotland the number of such admissions to the State
Hospital, Carstairs has fallen in the last decade, although in England the
reduction has been of a lesser magnitude (Robertson, 1982).[5] The effects of
accumulation over the years has meant that all the special hospitals (whatever their current admission policies) house a substantial number of patients
in the category of psychopathic disorder. If the maximum security hospitals
are disillusioned with psychopaths and their treatment, such disillusionment
is not difficult to understand. In short, their presence in large numbers, in
such hospitals, distorts that delicate balance which has to be struck between
treatment and security. Inevitably, for reasons of safety, the emphasis has
to be on security so that it becomes difficult to operate treatment regimens
which are designed to give patients increasing freedom and responsibility.
Fingers have been badly burned in the past, and most of the highly
publicised and notorious examples of maximum security patients re-
offending, either whilst in detention or after discharge, have involved
individuals with psychopathic disorders rather than those with psychotic
illnesses.

To summarise, those with anti-social personality disorders are not
generally welcomed in psychiatric hospitals. For non-offenders admission
to hospital, on those few occasions when it takes place, is likely to be as a
result of a transient situational disturbance and to be of limited duration.
There is even less enthusiasm for admitting psychopaths under compulsory
powers from the courts, although a few still are admitted to the special
hospitals. Therapeutic pessimism has been cited as the main factor which
discourages admission of these people to hospital but at least two other
factors are worthy of mention. The first is the basic psychiatric validity of
the concept of psychopathic disorder and the second is the problem of
predicting future behaviour in psychopaths.

Disagreement among psychiatrists is nothing new; indeed the fact that
there exists more than one school of psychiatric theory is frequently cited as
proof of the unscientific nature of the subject. This is not the place to argue
the point in general, but it does become relevant when a psychiatric diagnosis is given legal recognition. Such is the case in respect of psychopathic
disorder. Most people, including psychiatrists, would agree that some
individuals behave in a more persistently anti-social manner than others.
Does this in itself constitute a mental disorder? Is it merely the extreme end
of the spectrum of human social activity, or is it evidence of a mental
abnormality? Here there is the first disagreement. For those who take the
view that repeated anti-social behaviour indicates mental disorder, the only
psychiatric diagnosis that can be suggested is psychopathic disorder,

defined, inevitably, in terms of persistent anti-social behaviour. Thus the argument has been criticised, most cogently and famously by Lady Wootton (1978)[6] as a circular argument in which psychopathic disorder is defined in terms of anti-social behaviour, and then used to account for the behaviour. Other features have been considered necessary for the diagnosis; these have included an inability to feel for others or to recognise social obligations, and an inability to delay immediate gratification of needs. There is not good evidence that vague features such as these are capable of reliable measurement or rating, and in any case they are characteristics that come and go in all of us from time to time.

Attempts to identify a more scientific, or medical marker of psychopathic disorder have occupied an army of psychologists and psychiatrists over the years. Doubtless future generations will laugh at the efforts of twentieth-century psychiatrists in much the same way as we pour scorn on Lombroso's ideas of 100 years ago. A whole range of biological features have come under scrutiny since the shape-of-the-head theory of Lombroso fell from favour. Electro-encephalographic tracings, hormones, blood sugar levels, the composition of the sweat, the responsiveness of the autonomic nervous system, and chromosomes have all been measured and analysed with no conclusive evidence that any of them are causally related to the antisocial behaviour seen in psychopaths. We have to conclude that psychopathic disorder is a convenient, but medically dubious, term used to describe a group of people whose single distinctive feature is persistent anti-social behaviour. It has the legal accolade of recognition in the Mental Health Act when in fact it might be nothing other than wickedness. Indeed the Butler Report cites the view of one witness who 'saw the concept of psychopathic disorder as part of the general attempt of a secular society to replace moral explanations of behaviour by medico-scientific explanations'.

Statements such as this may be attractive in the debating arena but they ignore the one piece of crucial evidence that underpins the belief that some biological factor operates in the causation of psychopathic or criminal behaviour. This evidence relates to genetic studies which have been reviewed by Sarnoff Mednick and Barry Hutchings (1978).[7] Twin studies and adoption studies have been used in an attempt to investigate the extent to which psychopathic disorder results from inherited genetic factors as distinct from environmental factors operating in infancy and childhood. Identical twins share exactly similar types of genes whereas the genes of non-identical twins are no more alike than are those of ordinary siblings. There are a number of pitfalls in these studies, but there is certainly good evidence that for criminality there is a greater similarity (or concordance) among identical twins than there is between non-identical twins.

This finding would suggest that at least some inherited biological factors contribute to the causation of psychopathic disorder. Further confirmation comes from adoption studies which have demonstrated that the biological child of a criminal father (both of whom will share some common genetic characteristics) is more likely to be a criminal than is the adopted child of such a father. What is exactly transmitted by the genes, or how it produces its effects in antisocial behaviour remain a mystery.

With such controversy surrounding the category it is not surprising that it is applied by psychiatrists in a fashion that borders on the indiscriminate. Teenage gangsters, inadequate alcoholics, sexual deviants and sadistic murderers are all liable to have the diagnosis applied to them, with the result that as a diagnosis, it virtually loses all usefulness. Forensic psychiatrists, accustomed to seeing a range of offenders, tend to reserve the term for a rather narrow group of dangerously antisocial offenders, but even here there is no universal agreement. Undoubtedly the diagnosis creeps into countless psychiatric and social work reports, often making an indelible appearance in successive reports on the same individual. In this respect it carries a stigma which guarantees therapeutic despondency in all who assess the individual.

The poor results from treatment have been referred to earlier in this chapter and, for psychopaths admitted from courts, the aim of treatment is presumably to prevent antisocial behaviour occurring in the future. This involves prediction, which in the cases of psychopaths in the special hospitals, usually infers the prediction of dangerousness. This is yet another area of bitter controversy but for the moment let us limit our discussion to the special problems of predicting dangerousness in psychopaths as distinct from predicting dangerousness in for example psychotic patients. In the next chapter we will deal more generally with the topic of dangerousness.

In some rare situations a violent act may be the result of a psychotic illness. In other words the illness can bear a direct or causal relationship to the act. For example, a person suffering from paranoid schizophrenia might be convinced that his neighbours cause electricity to pass through his house, that they have planted microphone bugs in the wall and that they put poison in his food. Let us assume that under the influence of these ideas, he goes next door with a shotgun and murders his neighbour. In a straightforward case such as this, and assuming that there are no complicating factors, the dangerousness of the person is clearly related to his illness. If he can become well and free of his delusions he will not be dangerous, and so long as he remains well in the future he will not be dangerous. Moreover his illness is obvious and readily detectable. By careful assessment the experienced psychiatrist can gauge the intensity of the delusional beliefs and monitor their response to treatment. Also the patient's behaviour in hospital will provide invaluable information on the course of his illness. Does he think the hospital food is poisoned? Is he paranoid concerning other patients or his relatives? Does he recognise his behaviour as bizarre and does he appreciate the need to remain in treatment after leaving hospital? All these are questions that legitimately fall within the province of the psychiatrist because they relate unquestionably to identifiable mental illness.

The assessment of future dangerousness in psychopaths, particularly for those assessed in conditions of captivity, is very difficult. There are no gross signs of mental disturbance, as there are in the case of those suffering from psychotic illnesses, and the psychopath is able for long periods to conduct himself in a conforming manner. His appearance and conversation will be perfectly normal; indeed many psychopaths are highly skilled in presenting a façade of plausible normality to the outside world. The title *A Mask of Sanity* used by Harvey Cleckley (1964)[8] for his classical monograph of psychopathic disorders was well chosen. In these circumstances it is not surprising that psychiatrists are sometimes wrong in their predictions of dangerousness in psychopaths: there may be only slender medical evidence on which to form a judgement. Ultimately the assessor, be he psychiatrist, social worker or parole board member, is forced to rely on his own gut feelings to reach a conclusion. This may do a grave injustice to both the psychopathic offender (by failing to release him) or to society (by releasing him).

3 Offenders with alcohol and drug problems

Alcoholism is the commonest reason for men in Scotland to be admitted to a psychiatric hospital: twice as many men are admitted with this diagnosis than with any other single diagnosis. In women the number of such admissions is steadily rising. Sometimes the diagnosis of alcoholism is obvious on admission, but for many patients the diagnosis emerges following admission for a secondary psychiatric problem, such as neurotic anxiety or a depressive illness. Alcohol-related problems are extremely common in men admitted to general hospitals following overdoses, and there are also a number of specific psychiatric illnesses directly attributable to alcohol abuse. Some of these are sudden, relatively short-lived conditions, for example, delirium tremens and alcoholic hallucinosis. These illnesses usually make a fairly rapid response to treatment, but recurrence is very common. Other conditions are gradual in their onset and permanent in their effects. Most important amongst these is the condition of permanent brain damage due to alcoholism, known as Korsakov's Psychosis, which is seriously disabling as a result of the associated severe impairment of memory.

A vast amount of psychiatric hospital resources are, of necessity, devoted to the problems of alcohol abuse. This is perhaps a curious situation in that there is no unanimity of opinion within the medical profession that alcoholism is a disease at all. The debate about alcoholism affords many parallels with the earlier discussion on psychopathic disorder. For years, those who drank too much were simply regarded as morally weak but in the post-war period a strongly medical view which saw alcoholism as a disease was argued. This culminated in the much-quoted World Health Organisation definition of alcoholism which appeared in 1952. Alcoholics, it said,

> are those excessive drinkers whose dependence upon alcohol has attained such a degree that they show a noticeable mental disturbance or an interference with their mental and bodily health, their interpersonal relations and their smooth social and economic functioning; or who show the prodromal signs of such developments. They therefore require treatment.

This definition appears humane and forward looking, but from a medical viewpoint the last sentence from the World Health Organisation contains the sting in the tail. Thirty years later it is generally acknowledged that the psychiatric treatment of alcoholism has been a failure. Admission to a hospital (be it psychiatric or general) can give the alcoholic the chance to dry out; his liver and brain can take a rest from alcoholic assault. He may have the opportunity to take stock of his situation, his health, his marriage and his job. He may learn things about himself and about his addiction that he never knew before. But the likelihood that admission will successfully modify his drinking habits is, to put it at its best, very doubtful.

The medical view of alcoholism has in recent years given way to social theories which many observers find much more credible (Plant, 1982).[9] Emerging from social theories has come the forcefully argued suggestion (Kendell, 1979)[10] that the problem of alcoholism is essentially a political problem which the Government can deal with when ever it chooses to do so. Kendell has argued that problems due to alcohol abuse will diminish when the consumption of alcohol per head of the population falls from its current high level. One way of achieving this would be a policy of swingeing taxation. Needless to say the Government has responded by rejecting this politically unpopular remedy together with the theory from which it is derived (Health Departments of Great Britain and Northern Ireland, 1981).[11]

In summary psychiatry does not have, in the long term, a great deal to offer those with alcohol-related problems. Some units specifically for the treatment of alcoholism have developed; almost invariably admission to such a unit is on a voluntary basis. Nobody can be cured of alcoholism against his will and indeed good motivation is held to be a crucial ingredient for a successful outcome. Given this situation it is easy to see why, as in this survey, psychiatrists appear to offer so little to the offender with an alcohol problem. The provisions of the Mental Health Act are not appropriate for the admission to hospital of alcoholics, and there is a view that to detain someone in hospital compulsorily, on the grounds of alcoholism, would be a serious infringement of his liberty. It is for this reason that the Government has specifically excluded 'dependence on alcohol or drugs' from those conditions that qualify for compulsory admission (section 1, Mental Health Act 1983).

We have spoken in general terms of the difficulties in effectively treating alcoholism but we need to consider the special problems presented by offender patients with alcohol problems. While there is no doubt that a relationship exists between offending and excessive drinking, the precise nature of this relation remains far from clear. Just as alcohol abuse generates an enormous volume of work for medical facilities, so it does the same for the criminal justice and the penal systems. Statistics relating to convictions for drunkenness and for drinking and driving offences make gloomy reading but they are the tip of an iceberg. Unrevealed by the statistics will be countless other offences and crimes in which alcohol abuse has played a major part. These will range in their seriousness from the trivial, such as indecent exposure and prostitution, through property offences to the most serious cases of assault, rape and homicide. The one consistent finding to emerge from the many psychiatric studies of prison populations is that a large number of citizens are in prison, at least in part, as a result of drinking alcohol to excess. It cannot be assumed that they are all alcoholics, and even less readily should it be assumed that they would all warrant psychiatric treatment.

It is, of course, only a tiny minority of offenders who, as they pass through the criminal justice system, are referred for psychiatric assessment. In relation to alcohol-related offences there is quite likely to be a discrepancy between those whom the criminal justice officials choose to refer, and those whom the psychiatrists would see as the 'best-prospect-for-treatment' cases. For example, many crimes are committed as a direct result of the disinhibiting effects of alcohol; these may be of a minor nature, but they will also include some violent crimes often of a senseless and unusually brutal nature. The bizarre nature of the crime might precipitate a psychiatric referral, but the fact that an individual has been greatly disinhibited in his behaviour as a result of alcohol intoxication does not automatically mean he has a recurrent problem of alcoholism. Conversely an all too apparent problem of alcoholism is referred at a stage far beyond that at which any effective treatment is possible. The habitual drunken offender is a thorn in the flesh of the criminal justice system but by the time the habitual drunkard is an offender he is likely to have lost his job, his family and his home and to have accumulated enormous social problems. This background, with an absence of any supportive network in the community, militates against successful therapeutic intervention. Paradoxically it might well be that the best therapeutic prospects are never seen by psychiatrists. Drunken drivers were rarely referred for psychiatric assessment in this survey, but it is possible that this large group of offenders contains men whose social and occupational status are not so deteriorated as to overwhelm any treatment initiative. It would be foolish nonsense to pretend that everyone convicted of drunken driving is an alcoholic, but it is interesting to speculate why such a microscopic proportion of such offenders are sent to psychiatrists from the courts. Perhaps it is because so many regard drunken driving as an almost acceptable form of law-breaking; it causes little concern. The offenders appear manifestly normal, and their social and cultural backgrounds approximate more closely to those of the decision-makers in the criminal justice system than can be said for any other group of offenders. In this situation there is possibly a reluctance to invoke the help of a practitioner from the field of mental illness with all the attendant but unspoken fears and prejudices.

The specific problem of the habitual drunken offender requires a little further discussion. Technically the term 'habitual drunken offender' refers to those people who repeatedly appear in court on charges of being drunk in a public place. In practice related charges, such as those of being a vagrant or disturbing the peace, are commonly invoked. They are usually detained in custody overnight to appear in court the next morning. The majority, if convicted, are fined but as they are often unable to pay their fines they are then sent to prison for short periods. A leading article in the *British Medical Journal* (1982)[12] recently said:

> Everybody—policeman, magistrates, social workers, doctors, and prison and probation officers—agrees that this is a pointless, expensive, and time-consuming process: the offenders are not helped at all, and for most a court appearance and fine is no great punishment or even embarrassment.

Although there is agreement that our present method of dealing with drunken citizens is hopelessly inappropriate, the task of implementing something different is immense. An experimental detoxification centre in Edinburgh made no great impact (Hamilton *et al.* 1978)[13] on the problem, and the administrative will to co-ordinate an effort between the Home Office and the Department of Health and Social Security seems to be absent. A recent report from a multi-professional group under the chairmanship of Lord Donaldson (Federation of Alcoholic Rehabilitation Establishments, 1982)[14] proposed the establishment of community drying-out centres staffed by nurses and social workers with doctors providing an on-call service. The centres would receive all those who are at present charged with drunkenness and taken into custody; they would be managed according to social and medical needs as appropriate. Who can tell whether such an approach would have any more success than its predecessors? It seems tragic that money is wasted at present by processing drunken offenders in a way that is universally regarded as wrong. The police, the courts and the prisons are utilised, by default, for a function that they are ill-suited to perform. However, it is not simply a case of misdirected resources; even if the best facilities were available we cannot be sure that the problem is soluble. The habitual drunken offender is at first sight a problem of deceptive simplicity, but in fact it is a complex tangle with individual, social and medical elements. Throwing all the facilities known to mankind at it might not make it go away.

Much of the discussion concerning alcohol-related offending could be extended to offenders with problems of drug abuse. The manner of recording criminal offences conceals many crimes which are in fact drug-related. Thus an unknown number of robberies, frauds, housebreakings and thefts have a drug-obtaining motivation. Some crimes will be committed during a period of drug intoxication and then there are those offences which specifically relate to the possession of unlawful drugs. From a quantitative view the social, legal and medical problems that result from drug abuse are tiny in comparison with those associated with alcohol abuse. Individually the consequences of drug addiction can reach horrific scales, but the number of people with drug problems is insignificant compared with the number affected by alcohol abuse. There is clearly disproportionate media attention given to drug abuse, as compared with that given to alcohol addiction. The police seizure of the latest drugs cache at Heathrow Airport is front page news, while the steady consumption by the nation of increasing quantities of alcohol passes unnoticed. Indeed a vast amount of television advertising actually encourages the population to drink more beer and spirits in order to improve its manliness or sociability.

In the current survey, specific offences against any of the various Drug Acts accounted for less than one per cent of cases referred to psychiatrists by procurators fiscal. While alcoholism accounts for a fifth of all admissions to Scottish psychiatric hospitals, drug dependence accounted for less than one per cent of admissions in 1979. Indeed the relationship of medical practices to drug addiction is an interesting one. Not only does it appear that medical treatment has been ineffective in dealing with drug addiction, but it also seems that the prescribing habits of doctors might contribute in large measure to the very existence of the drug problem, if problem there be. An explosive increase in the number of drug addicts known to the Home Office occurred in the 1960s. These were principally young adults, who obtained their supplies directly from the rash over-prescribing of a handful of doctors, or indirectly when quantities of these lawfully prescribed drugs found their way on to the black market. The Dangerous Drugs Act of 1967 placed a statutory duty on doctors to notify the Home Office (not incidentally the Department of Health and Social Security which has responsibility for health matters) of any patient whom he suspects of being addicted to opiate drugs whether or not he is prescribing or indeed treating the addict. The Act also limited the prescribing of heroin and cocaine to a small number of specially licensed doctors practising from designated centres. Most of these National Health Service Drug Clinics are in London and they operate on an out-patient basis. What was the purpose of this approach? Firstly restricted prescribing was seen as a way of 'keeping out the Mafia' and controlling injudicious doctors. Addicts would have a legitimate source of clean drugs and would not need to shop around and thereby obtain impure, and potentially lethal, contaminated 'junk' on the streets. Secondly it was hoped that treatment from drug clinics would have a preventive component by curing individual cases and so prevent the 'spread factor' which is such an important feature in drug addiction.

These expectations, unfortunately, have not been met. Medical remedies are notoriously bad at changing life-styles, and the life-style of the drug addict has proved no exception. In relation to eliminating the black market, Dr Griffith Edwards (1979)[15] of the Institute of Psychiatry writes, 'The belief that competitive prescribing would prevent a black market has proved illusory. Responsible clinic prescribing by its very nature is conservative, and there is ample evidence that clinic attenders receiving maintenance opiates go on using drugs beyond those prescribed.' Whether or not the policy has succeeded in its preventive ideals is more difficult to say. What seems to have taken place is a change in the nature of drug abuse rather than a reduction. Instead of pure narcotic drug addiction, there is abuse of a whole range of analgesic, hypnotic, sedative and stimulant drugs most of which, although available only on a doctor's prescription, are easily obtainable. Dr Edwards concludes 'that a line has been held and things look less

threatening than in 1968, but yet in some ways preventive policies per-
severate on old problems and have not been updated to deal with current
realities. Preventive policies are still centrally designed around opiates, with
all else somehow regarded as secondary, and this is not a response which
accords with the dominant patterns of drug use that are now to be seen'.

If the elimination of the black market has not taken place, and prevention
has only been marginal, what effect has treatment policy had on delinquency among drug addicts? Again the hope was that regular prescribing of
drugs would eliminate the need for the addict to steal money, shoplift and
break into pharmacies and doctors' surgeries in order to obtain extra
supplies. Yet again the results are not simply hopeless, but they raise the
suggestion that treatment might even be counterproductive. In one of the
largest recent surveys of opiate addicts conducted in Britain, Wiepert *et al.*
(1979)[16] reported that treatment made no impact on the overall crime rate
among addicts but they 'found a change in the pattern of offences during
the treatment stage, with a significant *increase* (our italics) in the proportion
of drug offences. This increase in offences against drug legislation (the
majority of these offences involved opiates) at a time when our patients
were prescribed opiates during the course of treatment is contrary to
expectation.'

The appearance in the dock of a gaunt, ill-looking young man, dirty and
trembling, is a pathetic sight that naturally arouses compassion. The
medical risks to which these youngsters expose themselves are enormous
and many lives end prematurely. They clearly need help rather than punishment but it has to be acknowledged that the form of help which will enable
them to adjust to a normal existence, away from the drug scene, is presently
unknown to mankind. Sentencers may feel that a period of imprisonment
will at least provide the addict with a respite from drug-taking, and an
opportunity for his physical health to improve. Grapevine stories (which it
must be stressed have not been substantiated) suggest that even within
prison illicit drug-taking can occur.

4   The socially inadequate

Repeated offending within short periods of time, often accompanied by
repeated psychiatric referral, characterised this miscellaneous group of
offenders. The courts tended to regard them as nuisances, rather than as
dangerous and they posed a difficult problem for law-enforcement,
judicial, social and medical agencies. The term 'inadequates' is an unfortunate one, for it clearly has pejorative overtones, but the Butler Committee
felt obliged to use the term whilst acknowledging that it did so in a compassionate sense (*see also* 'Persistent Petty Offenders', Scottish Association for
the Study of Delinquency 1983).[17] The centres of most large conurbations
(Glasgow and Edinburgh in particular in Scotland) contain a core of homeless adults whose survival, in the absence of any support, is precarious.
Many have psychiatric disabilities such as chronic schizophrenia, mental

handicap, personality disorder or organic brain damage. A secondary problem of alcohol abuse is common, and virtually all of them will depend on institutional care variously provided by prison, mental hospital or common lodging house. As a group they tend to be inconsistent in their responses to caring agencies. Instead they exist on a day-to-day basis, with an unwillingness to settle for any lengthy period of time in one form of accommodation or another. Increasingly younger people and more females are swelling their ranks.

Locally they are usually well known to the police and their offending tends to be of a minor nature. Petty thefts (usually involving food), damage to property or disturbing the peace are the likeliest avenues into police custody, and some deliberately offend in order to obtain shelter in prison. Although there are few reliable statistics available, the problem appears to be increasing in size. It may simply be that public awareness of the 'inadequates' has increased at the same time as public tolerance for their eccentric behaviour has fallen. Simultaneously there has certainly occurred a reduction in the provision of appropriate sanctuary for this group of people. Reference has previously been made to the changing nature of psychiatric hospitals with the emphasis on an open-door policy and early discharge where possible. Years ago at least some of the 'inadequates' would have been cared for in mental hospitals on a long-term basis. They would have worked on the hospital-farm or in the laundry in the days when such hospitals were expected to be self-sufficient closed institutions. But all that has changed and today these individuals tend simply to leave hospital after a few days and rarely can their medical needs be such as to warrant compulsory hospitalisation.

Parallel with the reduction in mental hospital accommodation there has been a shrinkage in the availability of even the most basic forms of shelter in the community. Reception centres, common lodging houses and the provision of hostels by voluntary organisations have all undergone contractions and, in the face of competing demands on local authority finances, the homeless inadequate has found himself squeezed out. In this context the expression 'community care' is regarded by some as at best a fashionable catch-phrase, and at worst a sick joke. Dr Henry Rollin (1981)[18] in a critique of the demise of the large mental hospital writes:

> But for the country as a whole the field of community care is less green and less lush. Some of it is paved with good intentions but a large part is an arid waste which for lack of money and personnel has failed to be cultivated.

The 'inadequates' are an unrewarding group to deal with and their unattractiveness to the caring agencies doubtless contributes to their rejection. Police, court and prison personnel become exasperated by what they see as the totally inappropriate diversion of criminal justice facilities to deal with a group of offenders whose needs are in fact social and medical. Psychiatrists look to the community to provide proper care but the community is unable to do so. The problem is compounded by the unrealistic expectations that each service has of the other (Bluglass, 1980).[19] There is a failure not only of communication but also of professional understanding between the various groups and agencies involved. The Butler Committee concluded its discussion on the 'inadequates' by recognising that, at the end of the day, some individuals are simply not capable of being helped: '. . . we think that it may be right to accept, in the end, that the particular offender is not susceptible to rehabilitation by the efforts of the official agencies and that, apart from the courts imposing any penalties appropriate to the offences he may go on to commit, the official services can fulfil no useful purpose by continuing attempts to induce him to accept their help'.

Chapter 7

A Psychiatrist's Review of the Situation

The criminal justice system is concerned with the maintenance of law and order and the administration of justice. Medical services are concerned with the delivery of health care. Though both systems meet a public need, they differ widely from each other in their disparate functions and their manner of operation. The two systems are required to overlap in an area which for each system is a tiny fraction of their whole. Yet in this small area of overlap, represented by the mentally abnormal offender, are generated problems which pose fundamental questions for the police, the courts, the medical services, and the public which all these agencies serve. Only an alarmist would suggest that every day a large number of mentally abnormal offenders are the subjects of grave injustice at the hands of courts and hospitals. Equally it would be naive to imagine that each mentally abnormal offender is accurately identified and appropriately directed to a suitable disposal. The survey described in preceding chapters suggests that there are some areas of major concern and it is to those areas that this chapter addresses itself.

The police

Among his many other duties the police constable is required to attend to incidents of disturbed behaviour occurring in a public place or in a private dwelling if summoned. The nature of such disturbed behaviour is enormously varied, as are the reasons precipitating such behaviour. The policeman's duty may be seen as one of 'keeping the streets clean' and this seems to reflect public expectations. If the disorderly individual concerned cannot simply be taken home, as presumably many are, he can only be removed from the streets and legally detained in one of two places. The first is a police cell and the second is the ward of a psychiatric hospital. There is no other facility available and although the British Association of Social Workers have argued for the development of crisis intervention centres, it seems unlikely that any such centres will develop in the foreseeable future.

Psychiatric assistance will be sought for some of those people who come to the notice of the police in this way. As has been described in earlier chapters the method of summoning such assistance varies from area to area. A crucial distinction arises on the basis of whether or not the individual has been charged with an offence. If there is no police charge and the police escort the person to a centre for psychiatric assessment, then the hospital deals with the referral in exactly the same way as it would deal with any other emergency referral. That is to say, the person is examined and an assessment is made of whether or not he needs immediate psychiatric admission or some other form of psychiatric treatment or indeed no psychiatric treatment at all. Admission to hospital, and the legal terms of such admission, depend entirely on the clinical picture. The police have no on-going responsibility if the person is admitted to hospital and the responsibility of the hospital to the police, should the patient be admitted, is exactly the same as that which exists for all other patients of the hospital. This system, where it operates, has the advantage that it provides the police with immediate skilled psychiatric assessment. It can also reduce the instances of inappropriate detention in a police cell. On the other hand, some would argue that it is harmful, in a public relations sense, to have police cars and uniformed officers bringing disturbed individuals to the doors of a mental hospital at any hour of the day or night. Such activities could be disturbing for the patients of the hospital and upsetting for their relatives. A further difficulty is that at night psychiatric hospitals have low staffing levels and are relatively inactive as compared with the busy casualty departments of general hospitals in or near a city centre.

In those situations where the person has been charged with an offence the circumstances are altered. Here the arrested person is the 'property' of the police and though they might seek psychiatric or medical advice there can be no doubt that the responsibility for the safe custody of the person rests with them. The procedure adopted for the assessment of arrested persons is also subject to geographical variation. Depending on the local arrangements the examination of persons in custody is carried out either by a part-time police surgeon (usually a general practitioner) or by a psychiatrist who attends at the police station. For the 105 sample cases in which the police requested a medical examination, admission to a psychiatric hospital followed in sixty-two per cent of cases. This outcome was recommended in eighty-nine per cent of individuals examined by police surgeons, but in only thirty-eight per cent of those seen by psychiatrists. Clearly the psychiatrists are more selective, and the results have important implications. In City B the medical decision to remand in hospital is being made by a medical practitioner with no special psychiatric skills; he is not recognised under Section 27 of the Mental Health (Scotland) Act 1960 'as having special experience in the diagnosis and treatment of mental disorder'. It could be argued that as a general practitioner he is quite frequently required to admit an ordinary patient of his own to hospital under the civil powers of the Mental Health Act, and that his work for the police is essentially similar in nature to his every-day practice. The situations are, however, not quite similar, in that the civilly committed patient under Part IV of the Mental Health (Scotland) Act 1960 could be discharged by the responsible medical officer at any time. The remanded patient, however, presumably 'belongs' to the procurator fiscal and it would be difficult, if not impossible, for the responsible medical officer to discharge the patient from hospital without the prior agreement of the procurator fiscal. A further disadvantage of this system is that the police surgeon is not in a position to know the nature and extent of the facilities for the management of disturbed patients which exist in the local hospital. The psychiatrist on the other hand will be fully aware of what security exists in the hospital and will take this into consideration in arriving at his decision.

Perhaps the courts need to be made aware, particularly in relation to those individuals who might constitute a public danger, that a remand to hospital might be to a unit where there is no special security whatsoever. In such cases, if the paramount need is for safe custody then clearly prison would be a more appropriate place for the remand of the person than hospital would be. At one hospital it was made clear to the researchers that the responsibility, if remanded patients absconded, was seen as resting with the procurator fiscal and the police. The hospital undertook to do what it could to detain such patients but could give no assurances concerning the security of such detention. In other words, it was felt that the courts should only order a remand to hospital in those cases where absconding would not present any danger to the public. However, the feeling in other hospitals was that even though the responsibility might be the procurator's fiscal, the hospital had its own good name to preserve in the locality, and absconding remanded patients who caused problems in the neighbourhood would be seen by the public as the hospital's responsibility.

There is no doubt that the assessment in a police station of an acutely disturbed person, possibly under the influence of drugs or drink, is an exceedingly difficult task. It is most appropriately carried out by a psychiatrist who, in arriving at his disposal decision, will have knowledge of the hospital facilities that are available. Inappropriate admissions are to be avoided at all costs. They cause discontent in the hospital and are a disservice to the patient with possible long-term consequences: it is very easy to set in motion a chain of events on the basis of a short episode of disturbed behaviour which requires, for its resolution, nothing more than six hours' sobering-up.

Many of the comments made by members of the police force in Chapter 3 carried an assumption that serious violence was in some way a medical matter. Over half their requests for medical advice related to individuals demonstrating bizarre or violent behaviour and reference has been made to the tendency automatically to regard inexplicable behaviour as being the result of mental illness. It should be stressed that, where violence is concerned, this is rarely the case; situational factors and the effects of alcohol are much more likely causes than is the presence of a mental illness. It is, however, recognised that the police often have to operate under very difficult circumstances and they are publicly vulnerable. The public demands high standards from the police and expects them to deal appropriately with a wide range of disturbed individuals. Disorderly behaviour in the streets must be mopped up but at the same time the police are expected to divert into a medical channel those who are sick and in need of care. The task is a difficult one for a profession that receives no training in the identification of mental illness, and for one that sees as its principal task the prevention and detection of serious crime. The fact that two out of every three people they refer to a doctor are later admitted to a mental hospital suggests that the police are exercising skilled judgement in the matter.

If it is acknowledged that the consequences of the inappropriate detention of mentally ill persons in custody are serious, and that the police are in a highly vulnerable situation, then it follows that the police should have ready access to sound medical and social work assistance at all hours of the day and night. They are entitled to receive, on a twenty-four-hour basis, the best possible, skilled psychiatric advice that is available. It is recognised that this raises problems of manpower for psychiatric services in the National Health Service, but on the other hand applying the expensive criminal justice system to petty offenders with major mental illnesses is a costly nonsense.

Prosecution

A second opportunity for a psychiatric intervention occurs at the point of prosecution, when it may be initiated by the procurator fiscal or public prosecutor. In practice psychiatric reports are mandatory for those charged with murder but they are discretionary in all other classes of crimes. The procurator fiscal is essentially concerned with the arrested person's fitness to be prosecuted. He must decide whether or not there is sufficient excuse for the conduct of the accused person to warrant the abandoning of proceedings against him. Such a judgement naturally requires consideration in the light of public concern or interest in the particular case.

The procurator fiscal is dependent on information contained in the papers submitted to him by the police and in some situations he will have with these papers the results of a medical examination if this has been carried out on the accused while in police custody. Attention has been drawn to the relatively large number of recommendations for psychiatric hospital admission made by general practitioners working as part-time police surgeons. Such recommendations take the form of advice to the procurator fiscal (and thence the court) that the accused be remanded by the court to a psychiatric hospital for further assessment and, where necessary, treatment. This facility, for the diversion of some offenders to hospital early in the prosecution process, is attractive but it is not without problems. The most important of these, as indicated previously, is that advice is being taken from a doctor who is not fully conversant with the facilities of the local mental hospital and who himself has no specialised psychiatric expertise. The right of a hospital consultant to decide which patients are, and which patients are not, admitted under his care is jealously guarded. The remand to hospital of compulsory patients upon the advice of non-psychiatrically qualified doctors may be the source of misunderstandings between courts and hospitals. A series of questionable decisions escalated into a 'sequence of misunderstandings and, as the tragic outcome shows, misjudgements and shortcomings', as described by Scottish Secretary of

State, George Younger, in the House of Commons (Hansard, 1980)[1] following a triple murder in Glasgow in February of that year. This case occurred during the course of the current survey. It highlights many areas of difficulty and is therefore worth describing in some detail.

James Harkins, a twenty-nine-year-old Glasgow mortuary attendant was charged with attempted murder, assault and a breach of the peace. The charges arose out of his attempts to 'snatch' his four-year-old son from his estranged wife's care at a crêche at his wife's place of work (Gartnavel Royal Hospital in Glasgow). After arresting Harkins the police requested that he be examined by a police surgeon and this resulted in a recommendation that he be remanded to a mental hospital. Thus at his first court appearance Harkins was remanded to Woodilee Hospital for one week for further medical reports. He appeared again in court on 15 January 1980 and medical reports stated that he was sane and fit to plead, and that he no longer required hospital treatment. An application for bail was refused, and for reasons that remain unclear Harkins was recommitted by a sheriff to Woodilee Hospital. This committal was clearly not warranted on medical grounds but nonetheless the hospital admitted Harkins in compliance with the judicial order.

Mr Younger noted that the hospital staff were not 'clear about what was expected of them by this re-committal. The psychiatrist taking responsibility for Mr Harkins' case states that he telephoned the procurator fiscal's office for information about the reason for Mr Harkins' return and was promised further information when the appropriate official was contacted. The procurator fiscal's staff have no record of the receipt of such a call.'

The police had categorised Harkins (while he was in their custody) as a special risk prisoner with a history of violence and attempted suicide, and a form indicating this was sent with the remanded man to hospital. In Woodilee Hospital Harkins, whose mental condition within the hospital had not given any cause for concern, was placed in an open ward and allowed ground parole. On 5 February 1980 he absconded from the hospital grounds and made his way to Glasgow Royal Infirmary where he removed a scalpel from a locked cabinet. He then travelled by taxi to Gartnavel Royal Hospital where he stabbed, in the hospital crêche, his son, his wife and his brother-in-law.

Mr Younger, in his Parliamentary written reply, drew attention to three important links in the chain of errors that led to the tragedy. Firstly he criticised the sheriff court for the misunderstanding which resulted in Harkins' re-committal to hospital when the psychiatric report (for which Harkins had been remanded to hospital in the first instance) did not recommend such a course of action. Secondly he was critical of the staff of Woodilee Hospital for according Harkins the freedom which enabled him to leave the hospital environs unhindered. Although the re-committal to hospital was in error, Mr Younger felt that the hospital had a duty to keep Harkins under close supervision until the matter was clarified. Finally the Scottish Secretary drew attention to the lack of a sense of urgency shown by the nursing staff in response to Harkins absconding from the hospital grounds.

These criticisms are perhaps predictable and they were followed by the announcement of certain procedures designed to prevent the possibility of any further misunderstandings, and a requirement that in future no prisoner remanded to a mental hospital be allowed freedom to wander in the hospital grounds. Of equal importance however are the unanswered questions that remain from the Harkins affair and the problems they exemplify. It is relevant to record as a postscript to the tragic story that, whatever Harkins' mental condition may or may not have been on the day of the murders, he was considered by the court sane and fully responsible for his actions in law. Thus he was convicted of murder, not the lesser charge of culpable homicide, and received the mandatory sentence for such a crime, namely life imprisonment.

We might ask why, at the time of Harkins' first arrest, it was thought necessary to summon a police surgeon to examine his mental condition. He had been arrested on a charge of violence towards his family; not an unusual occurrence in Glasgow, but what was special in this case that required the attention of a doctor? What led the police surgeon to decide (according to the newspaper reports—*Daily Telegraph*, 9 April 1980) that 'this man is psychotic and unfit to plead and arrangements have been made for him at Woodilee'? Within a few days the consultant psychiatrist at Woodilee Hospital was able to conclude that Harkins was sane and fit to plead, and that he did not require hospital care. Was it ever clinically appropriate for the man to have been admitted to a hospital in the first instance? If he had been examined in the police station by a psychiatrist, instead of by a police surgeon, would a recommendation for his remand to hospital have been made?

Further questions arise in relation to the level of understanding between the court and the hospital. The court remanded the prisoner to Woodilee Hospital on two occasions and the second of these followed an application for bail which the same court refused. Was the court aware that Harkins might be (in fact was) treated in an open ward of a hospital with no secure facilities? When Harkins was remanded to Woodilee on the second occasion were the staff of that hospital aware that a bail application had been refused? The answers to these questions are matters for speculation but the questions illustrate that, not only is communication between court and hospital poor, but also that each has very little understanding of the working practices of the other.

The principle of remanding a defendant to a psychiatric hospital for the purpose of examination is an excellent one. It allows the making of a comprehensive assessment of the accused on the basis of twenty-four-hour observation by skilled medical and nursing staff. It has great advantages over the snapshot assessment of a defendant that a psychiatrist has to make when he examines such a person in prison. But if the system of remanding a defendant to hospital is to work satisfactorily, certain safeguards must be established. The court must be confident that the accused can be remanded to hospital and reliably detained there until he is next required to appear in court. The hospital staff must be confident that they have the proper facilities for managing the patient according to his clinical need. They must appreciate the requirement to detain him safely throughout the period of remand. It thus follows that the court should only remand an accused person to hospital when the recommendation for such a remand is made by the consultant psychiatrist who will have charge of that patient during the period of his hospital remand. It can be assumed that the consultant will have previously discussed the case with his nursing staff in order to ensure that proper facilities exist for managing the patient. It is unreasonable, and perhaps unsafe, to expect hospital staff to detain and treat a patient when none of them has had an opportunity to advise on the suitability of that patient for admission.

No psychiatric hospital provides special facilities solely for remand purposes, and it would clearly be inappropriate to remand certain defendants facing serious charges to an ordinary mental hospital, however useful such a period of hospital observation would prove. In such cases it might be that more use could be made of the facilities at the special (maximum security) hospitals such as Broadmoor Hospital in England or the State Hospital in Scotland, where the security is of such a high order. The view could be held that a pre-trial remand to a special hospital might jeopardise the outcome of the trial for the accused. Although there is evidence that remands in custody more often result in conviction than do remands on bail, there has been no research on the outcome of court proceedings for those defendants who are remanded to special hospitals. To date the number of such cases is very small.

In Scotland requests for pre-trial psychiatric assessments issue from the procurator fiscal and are directed to a named psychiatrist (usually the physician superintendent) at the local psychiatric hospital. The manner in which these requests are allocated to various consultants on the staff of the hospital depends upon the internal policies of that hospital. The matter is of more than academic interest. Most hospitals operate an internal system of regionalisation with each consultant taking responsibility for a defined geographical area. When the question arises of admitting a patient from court, then the doctor making such a recommendation to the court will be the consultant responsible for the sector in which that particular patient resides. What is more important is the fact that he will also be the consultant carrying out treatment in the event of the patient's admission to hospital. This seems entirely proper and in accordance with the understandable wish of consultants to control their own admissions. However, the other side of the coin means that the outcome depends largely, if not in total, on the view of one doctor. If he considers the defendant does not warrant a psychiatric disposal, then it is highly unlikely that any other consultant will be able to effect this. In discussing a different, but related, topic Dell (1980)[2] likened the situation to a 'feudal system, with each sector team reigning over its own strip and outside authorities, regional and national, unwilling or unable to interfere'.

To the observer, the discretion introduced into the criminal justice system by the request for a psychiatric report is bewildering. First there is the prosecution's discretion in ordering the psychiatric report. 'Odd behaviour', 'the feel of the case', 'a good holding situation' were all reasons advanced by procurators fiscal for obtaining reports. There can be no possibility of a psychiatric disposal in those cases that do not even come to the attention of a psychiatrist. The procurator fiscal refers such a tiny proportion of his cases for psychiatric assessment that it is difficult to understand how that tiny minority differs from the larger group of which they form part. The task confronting the fiscal is essentially one of a practical nature: a large number of cases to be processed in a short space of time and under considerable pressure. It would be understandable if the cases referred to psychiatrists simply represented a group with the common characteristic of being problem cases. The nature of the problem might be varied, but shunting the case into a psychiatric siding (at least temporarily) buys a little time while less problematical cases are processed. It is difficult to conceive of any scientific selection that determines the referral of cases by the prosecution to a psychiatrist. He may be asked to see the violent or the chronic drinkers, but in reality the great majority of violent offenders or alcoholic offenders are never referred for an opinion.

If the discretion of the procurator fiscal has an inscrutable quality, so too has that of the psychiatrist. If the results of this study are taken at face value they appear logical and consistent. Thus offenders who are diagnosed as mentally ill are, by and large, offered hospital admission and others, including the personality disordered, are referred back to the court for a penal disposal. Such a conclusion ignores the fact that the diagnosis to a great extent determines the recommendation. Having made the diagnosis of mental illness the examining psychiatrist is almost under a professional (and perhaps a moral) obligation to offer treatment. Yet this obligation can be avoided by making an alternative diagnosis which does not carry the implication of treatment. It is certainly true that many of the patients who appeared in the study had dual, even multiple diagnoses. For example transient episodes of psychosis (mental illness) were not uncommonly found in the setting of personality disorder. The cynic might observe that by emphasising one aspect or another of the diagnostic picture, the psychiatrist can manipulate the 'treatability' of the case and thereby alter his professional obligation. Unrewarding or clinically unattractive patients are welcomed by few psychiatrists and many mentally abnormal offenders fall into these categories. It is easy to see how subtle processes can operate in the assessment of the offender, which lead the psychiatrist to diagnose an untreatable condition and accordingly reject the patient.

Whatever factors may operate in the selection of cases by the procurator fiscal for psychiatric referral, and in their subsequent filtering by the psychiatrists, approximately thirteen per cent of referred cases were ultimately admitted to hospital. This figure is very similar to that reported by Bowden (1978)[3] in a study of men remanded in custody for medical reports in Brixton Prison.

After conviction

Decision-making in the final stage of the criminal justice system rests with the sentencer. To him falls the task of disposing of the case in a way that meets the requirements of natural justice, and at the same time offers the public some protection and the offender some hope of reform. The task is not an easy one in respect of any offender. In the case of the mentally abnormal offender it may be well nigh impossible. The sentencer's discretion is wide and he has an ever-expanding range of disposal options available to him. Among these are some disposals which may be said to be psychiatric in nature (see Chapter 2). They vary from an order for hospital admission to a recommendation for voluntary out-patient treatment. Whatever the nature of the psychiatric disposal, the key to such a disposal is the opinion of the psychiatrist. There can only be a psychiatric disposal when it is recommended by a psychiatrist and it can only be recommended in cases that are referred to a psychiatrist for examination by the sentencer. Once again the discretionary factors in these two areas is of crucial importance.

In calling for psychiatric reports, sheriffs in Scotland seemed much influenced by the nature of the offence and a previous history of psychiatric illness in the defendant. These same considerations applied at the earlier stage of prosecution but a third factor, namely alcohol-related offending, also operated at the sentencing stage. Not surprisingly it seemed that most psychiatric cases had been filtered out earlier in the criminal justice process, and only ten per cent of cases referred by sheriffs resulted in hospital admission. A further twelve per cent received out-patient care as a condition of probation and over a third of this latter group comprised men convicted of sex offences. The sentencer may be forgiven for feeling that it is his unhappy lot to select the least inappropriate disposal from a range of options, each of which, for one reason or another, provides a less than satisfactory solution. Nowhere is this more true than in cases relating to chronic petty offenders with problems of alcohol abuse. Unsuitable for supervision or probation, for community service or for hospital admission, such individuals inevitably swell the ranks of the prison population.

Conclusion

Something like four out of five psychiatric reports ordered by procurators fiscal or sheriffs do not result in an offer of psychiatric treatment. The time expended in the preparation of these reports, their financial cost, and the loss of freedom for defendants remanded in custody for them, are not insignificant. Why is there such an apparent incongruity between that which the court expects and that which psychiatrists deliver? Perhaps the single underlying answer is that the criminal justice system is the wrong machine to introduce a potential patient to a medical facility. By tradition medical treatment is provided on the basis of clinical need; the sole determinant of treatment is the particular clinical condition of the individual. These same principles operate in relation to psychiatric treatments, and in only ten per cent of patients admitted to psychiatric hospitals are the laws of civil commitment invoked to provide the treatment. Even for these patients compulsory admission is more likely to be utilised to prevent harm befalling the patient than to protect society (Chiswick, 1980).[4] But when the court is minded to order a psychiatric disposal it is considering not only the welfare of the offender, but also the demands of natural justice and, on occasions, the protection of the public. It is these additional considerations that so alter the manner of the patient's inception into psychiatric care and the psychiatrist's terms of reference in relation to him.

In seeking a psychiatric disposal for an offender the court will be hoping that treatment will help the offender and stop him offending again. If the psychiatrist is principally concerned with the offender's mental condition and the likelihood of its being improved by treatment, then he and the court may be at cross purposes in their dialogue. This particularly applies when the link between the offence and the psychiatric abnormality is tenuous. These conflicting aims can have an outcome that appears puzzling to court, psychiatrist and public. For example, the psychiatrist might recommend committal to hospital for an offender who has committed some minor breach of the peace, but who suffers from a psychiatric illness of some severity. The court may feel that detention in hospital is too severe a penalty for what is only a minor infringement of the law, but the psychiatrist is making a recommendation on the basis of the offender's requirement for treatment, not on the seriousness of his offending. Alternatively a persistent sex offender whose offending, though not dangerous, constitutes a serious public nuisance may be offered out-patient treatment by the psychiatrist. The court is really wanting the sex offender put away, but the psychiatrist sees no medical indication for in-patient care and he offers what he thinks is appropriate on clinical grounds. Sometimes the court's confidence in the psychiatrist's wisdom may be severely shaken, as for example when the psychiatrist suggests out-patient or voluntary treatment for an offender who, on public policy grounds, must receive a custodial sentence. Such cases cause intense irritation to sentencers yet they are understandable in terms of the conflicting aims of court and doctor. Clearly the wise psychiatrist will be sensitive to the probable attitude of the court to the particular offender, and he will pitch his recommendation accordingly. One way round the dilemma is for the psychiatrist to offer out-patient treatment to the offender on a voluntary basis, after the court has disposed of the case and any sentence has been served.

The public attitude to the detention of patients in psychiatric hospitals is curiously ambivalent. There is indignation and outrage at shortcomings and blunders that result in the escape of dangerous patients (as for example in the case of James Harkins discussed earlier in this chapter), or in the premature discharge of patients who later re-offend. At the same time a series of public revelations of mental hospital scandals and the lobbying activities of various pressure groups have combined to produce an attitude of less than wholehearted public confidence in the psychiatric profession. Indeed this attitude is apparent in the Governmental White Paper which preceded the introduction of the Mental Health Act 1983. The first listed objective of that Act was to 'improve safeguards for detained patients' and the Act introduced unprecedented measures to limit the power of doctors to carry out certain forms of treatment on detained patients and also, to a lesser extent, on voluntary patients (Department of Health and Social Security *et al.,* 1981).[5] Such attitudes may or may not be justified but it would be surprising if they did not play some part in shaping the courts' view of psychiatric disposals. The probable effect is simply to discourage requests for psychiatric reports on those offenders whose offence appears too trivial to merit compulsory admission to hospital.

If the court considers indefinite detention in a mental hospital too draconian a measure for some offenders, there may be other offenders for whom the court views lengthy incarceration in hospital as a particularly attractive form of disposal. Indeed committal to hospital under the terms of a hospital order (perhaps with an additional order restricting discharge) is the only form of indeterminate sentence available, other than life imprisonment, for adult offenders. The use of life imprisonment is virtually confined to those convicted of murder (for whom it is mandatory) although it can be imposed for manslaughter, rape, buggery, incest and unlawful intercourse with a girl aged less than thirteen years. In fact it is hardly ever imposed for these latter offences, whereas a hospital order can be imposed for any offence, other than murder, punishable by imprisonment. Thus while it is true that the court may see indefinite detention in hospital as too drastic for some offenders, it might equally see it as the ideal for others. The psychiatric disposal is clearly vulnerable to these dual concerns for individual liberty on the one hand, and for public protection on the other.

Psychiatric vulnerability is nowhere more starkly demonstrated than it is in relation to the special provision made in the Mental Health Act 1959 for mentally disordered individuals who are deemed dangerous. There is no special sentence available to the court for disposing of offenders who may be dangerous. The sentencing judge will no doubt form a view of the offender's dangerousness, and this view will be reflected in the sentence he chooses to impose. The sentence however can only be within the tariff for that particular offence; the judge only has power to select a sentence within the limits laid down by law. The effect is that the dangerous offender (unless he is convicted of murder) will usually receive a prison sentence of determinate length. For the mentally disordered offender who is deemed dangerous the situation is altered in two crucial respects. If the court decides to impose a hospital order, it can acknowledge the dangerousness of the offender firstly by adding an order restricting discharge (a restriction order), and secondly by committing him to a special hospital of maximum security (see Chapter 2). Thus it is that dangerous mentally disordered offenders can be indefinitely incarcerated in conditions of security, while dangerous mentally normal offenders can only receive the sentence laid down by law. There can be little doubt that for the majority of offenders, the time spent in detention in a special hospital is longer than it would have been had they received a prison sentence for the identical offence.

The assessment, treatment and prediction of dangerousness are all highly contentious issues (Hamilton and Freeman, 1982).[6] Observers find it difficult to agree on a definition of dangerousness, and assessments made by different professionals show a high level of discordance. Finally, the matter of predicting the future behaviour of people designated dangerous is a task that borders on the impossible. These problems are all well recognised by researchers in criminology. Indeed the Butler Committee, in its discussion of dangerousness and its prediction, quoted the 1969 Report of the Parole Board which said:

> Despite every care in the process of selection, the imposition of conditions, and the supervision of paroled offenders, serious lapses must be expected to occur occasionally . . . notwithstanding the greatest care and judgement, there can be no certainty in the prediction of human affairs.

What is of concern in the context of the mentally disordered offender is that, despite all the uncertainties and difficulties, there exists under mental health legislation a form of preventive detention which is not available for any other class of offender. This state of affairs is partly historical in origin but it also depends in large measure on the publicly held belief, in fact a myth, that society has more to fear from the mentally disordered dangerous offender than it has from his mentally normal, but nonetheless dangerous, counterpart. Perhaps these are fine distinctions of only academic interest and of little practical importance. The late Sir Denis Hill, for so long the doyen of British psychiatry, referred to a dichotomy of views held by the British public in relation to mentally abnormal offenders (Hill, 1982).[7] What he called the 'soft left' was concerned with the protection of civil and human rights but the 'hard right' 'is not particularly interested in human rights and believes that the psychotic homicide case, the arsonist, and the child molester are inherently evil and should either be eradicated or confined for life'.

The importance of public attitudes in relation to the mentally abnormal offender, whether those attitudes are based on fact or fiction, can never be disregarded. There seems good evidence (Bluglass, 1978)[8] that a combination of public and professional attitudes has thwarted the development of the Regional Secure Unit programme recommended in the Butler Report of 1975 and thereafter adopted as Governmental policy in England and Wales, though not in Scotland. Progress in establishing these units has been painfully slow and has met with resistance in the form of professional suspicion and public fear. The Butler Committee envisaged a programme to provide 1000 beds in conditions of medium security on a regional basis throughout England and Wales. More significantly, it was hoped that the Regional Secure Units would be regarded as the hub for the development of regional forensic psychiatric services. The policy comprised much more than the provision of secure accommodation; it included the need for an investment in personnel who would provide assessment, advisory and treatment facilities for mentally abnormal offenders, and also for non-offender patients whose mental disorders required treatment in some degree of security. It was also hoped that the units would become centres for training and research within the speciality of forensic psychiatry. Such hopes remain unrealised in England and Wales, and in Scotland the whole programme has been rejected by the Scottish Home and Health Department as one not appropriate for the needs of the mentally disordered in that country.

These are matters of regret. The results of this survey demonstrate that the processing of the mentally abnormal offender through the criminal justice system is something of a random affair. The selection of cases for referral to a psychiatrist, and his selection of cases for treatment are matters largely of discretion, and a host of factors unrelated to the clinical need of the offender may distort the process. But it does seem that the mechanisms function most effectively where there are psychiatric staff cognizant of, and sympathetic to the needs of this special group of patients. Problems are compounded when police, prosecutors, doctors and sentencers fail to appreciate each others' working practices, and when they fail to communicate effectively with one another. Special facilities or units may, or may not, provide some answers. What seems more urgent however is a shift in public and political attitudes which will allow the diversion of a large number of offenders away from the arrest and prosecution process, and the provision of basic care in the community for them. The expectations that one group has of another require clarification, and research is necessary to evaluate alternative strategies within the criminal justice system for those mentally abnormal offenders who cannot be diverted from it.

Chapter 8

Future Possibilities

This study set out to fulfil two requirements: (1) to make a detailed research study at the arrest and prosecution stages in Scotland, and (2) to consider a number of wider issues relating to mental abnormality and crime within criminal justice processes generally. In looking to future possibilities it is appropriate to consider them separately under each of those headings, the former being the more specific and short-term and arising directly from the Scottish research study, while the latter deals more generally with issues relating to the interface between criminal justice processes and medical services and is thus more speculative and long-term.

1 The Scottish situation

The research study showed clearly that the law relating to mental illness or abnormality provides only the general framework in which social action and decision-making take place, and that what actually occurs in individual cases depends to a very large extent on local traditions, the views of key personnel in the local police force, the prosecuting department, the courts, and the medical and psychiatric services in the locality. Of crucial importance also was, of course, the availability of various kinds of medical and psychiatric facilities. Variations in the different regions within the country were often substantial, but it is perhaps helpful to set out in a summary form the answers to the questions which were raised at the beginning of the research study:

1 **What action do the police take when they suspect that an arrested person may be mentally deranged?**

   Advice is sought from a general practitioner or a police surgeon (save in one city where psychiatrists are available) as to fitness to be detained and an examination is carried out in police cells. Police records are checked as a matter of routine, and some information is obtained from hospital records on occasion.

2 **Are mental health doctors prepared to attend at the cells for examination of such persons?**

   In City A, yes; in other areas only in emergencies.

3 **Are facilities available to take such persons to hospital immediately?**

   In City A, should the examining psychiatrist decide that immediate

94

hospital admission is necessary, he will arrange accordingly. In City B there is an arrangement whereby beds must be made available if police surgeons wish hospital admission on remand. Otherwise doctors wishing emergency admission or admission on remand must themselves find the hospital willing to admit.

4 Is the procurator fiscal consulted about such cases?

Not always before removal to hospital, especially in relation to minor offending, but procurators fiscal are available for consultation by police on a round-the-clock basis should any doubts arise and they are always consulted in cases of serious crime.

5 Do the police report their suspicions, and any action taken, to the procurator fiscal in cases where the accused is kept in custody?

Yes, such information is a normal part of police reports.

6 If they do, what action does the procurator fiscal then take?

This is a matter for individual cases and individual procurators fiscal, but if police information indicates possible psychiatric problems, then the procurator fiscal can ask for a remand for psychiatric reports at the first court appearance, or, occasionally, he can mark a case 'no proceedings'.

7 Are the courts prepared to send accused to hospital on remand, rather than to prison, and are there adequate hospital facilities for such remands?

The court must be sure that a hospital bed is available. This means that medical advice in some form must already have been obtained and a hospital must be willing to admit. While courts are prepared to remand to hospital when so advised, issues of serious crime and dangerousness may over-ride other considerations because of lack of hospital security. Also hospitals are in general only willing to accept certain types of cases.

The brief answers to the specific questions naturally need to be placed in the context of the national and local constraints and pressures on the various decision-makers. Of course, before any action can be taken which appertains to mental illness or disorder, the respective control agency—the police, the prosecutor or the judge—has to have decided, on a commonsense basis, that the offender, or alleged offender, is *apparently* suffering from some mental illness or disorder so that an expert medical diagnosis can be obtained. The research indicated that on that commonsense basis of recognition of mental abnormality some offenders slip through the net and are not at the time referred for expert advice. This would indicate the need for some form of medical guidelines or the provision of some information during training so as to alert law-enforcement and criminal justice personnel as to signs that might suggest the need to seek a medical opinion, thus providing specialist advice in taking the responsibility on issues of fitness to detain, fitness to be prosecuted, i.e. to stand trial, and fitness for the imposition of ordinary penal sanctions. However, the research also indicates that there is a lack of medical facilities for dealing with the offenders who may present a problem of security to the authorities and that medical facilities are not generally available for the petty offender, especially those with a persistent pattern of minor offences or a history of alcoholism. They are not wanted in mental hospitals which now have an open-door policy.

There was found to be a tension between the police and medical practitioners, because the police see that medical specialists 'choose' their cases and leave the difficult, and violent offenders, as well as the petty or persistent offenders who appear mentally unstable, to the ordinary processes of law enforcement and criminal justice. This problem is not peculiar to Scotland and the following view of a Police Chief in the USA is one that would be reiterated by many in Great Britain.

> The trouble with being a cop is you get all the dirty jobs no one else will touch. . . . Take psychos . . . the hospitals won't take them, the doctors don't even want to talk to them, the relatives have given up trying. We are all that's left. . . . Next thing you know we've got lawyers and doctors . . . screaming about civil rights and us cops keeping sick people in jail.'[1]

There is consequently in Scotland an often expressed hope for the provision of Crisis Intervention Centres, or Services and Special Bail Hostels for the main urban areas, in order to cope more effectively with mentally abnormal accused persons at the early stages of the criminal justice process.

At the sentencing stage there are also considerable difficulties relating to the use of specific measures for the mentally abnormal offender. Here again it is not just a question of medical diagnosis but a survey to assess the potential of medical treatment in terms of current psychiatric thinking. Psychiatric hospitals do not have to deal with mentally abnormal offenders sent to them from the courts, they deal with those they *choose* to treat from the selection offered to them through the courts. Admissions to mental hospitals, including even the State Hospital with maximum security, can only be from the courts on the *recommendation* of psychiatrists in the light of current psychiatric thinking. The hospitals are reluctant to take the mentally disordered offender who may be disruptive, or the drunkard who is likely to be disruptive and not amenable to medical treatment. In this respect it is the personnel of the medical services that control criminal justice decisions and not vice versa. Few special provisions for *secure units* in mental hospitals are available in Scotland and at present there does not appear to be any serious consideration being given to development in that area. For some years now in England and Wales it has been accepted policy to establish *secure units* but very slow progress has so far been made in that direction. Consequently, many of the offenders whose behaviour and attitudes are, to say the least, noticeably bizarre now make up a not insignificant part of the population in Scottish as well as English prisons. The conclusion of an English survey carried out some fifteen years ago would seem to be true today for the whole of the United Kindom: 'There must be a serious reappraisal of the potency of present-day psychiatric procedures. It is my opinion that the tools of psychiatry are still blunt and primitive and in fact are largely ineffectual when used on the general body of mentally abnormal offenders we are called upon to treat.'[2]

This research indicated that many of those responsible for criminal justice decision-making are not fully aware of current psychiatric thought and practice. Psychiatric thinking in the 1960s was that not only could advice be given to the criminal justice system about offenders with mental problems, but also that a solution could be given: psychiatrists took a wide view of their remit and would accept the alcoholic, the sex offender, the personality-disordered who 'belonged' to medicine rather than to criminal justice. Now things are out of step. The criminal justice system has come to accept the wider view of the offender's responsibility and seeks to make the psychiatrist accept the responsibility for that offender's care. But since then psychiatry itself has changed. Mental hospitals now seek to provide treatment and cure rather than containment, and many of the problem offenders are no longer considered as being treatable. The knowledge of those in the criminal justice system needs to be brought up-to-date in this respect.

Within the medical profession in Scotland there are different perspectives as regards the relationship between criminality and mental abnormality and possible treatment strategies; but a document setting them out in relation to facilities could go a long way in dispelling doubt and dealing with difficulties.

The research study has indicated the large group of petty recidivists and alcoholics who come to police attention. The hospitals have already tried to help many of them, but perhaps through lack of self-motivation they have failed to be helped and they come back to court and prison. Currently prisons attempt to perform a social/medical role for these offenders and when released they are sobered, cleaned, fit and fed, only to offend again. There is a growing acceptance that rehabilitation is not possible. Is the prison role to be a social one? But if the need is social, why prison? And if detoxification or similar centres are to be the answer, then resources ought to be made available by the government from public funds.

Similar arguments are involved, but at perhaps a more serious level, where the personality-disordered offenders are concerned. Treatment is no longer considered possible; psychiatric hospitals are not the place for them. Scarce resources must be used primarily for those who can be treated or cured.[3] A case is made for the 'asylum' role of the prison where care and security can be combined. Such a development may be considered as in line with 'positive custody' as outlined in the May Report.[4] On the other hand, numbers must be remembered, and twenty per cent of the court sample were diagnosed as suffering from a 'personality disorder' which would mean some 350 from the total group for whom psychiatric advice was sought.

Regional secure units are not proposed in Scotland, and if mental hospitals are not the place for them, then this group must be taken into account in the continuing debate as to the role of prisons in future and perhaps brought under special regimes in the prison system. Again, these issues can involve resources, and hence taxation and government policy. The continuation of the present situation places an extreme burden on prison resources, especially on staff who are not trained to cope with cases of mental abnormality.

These are issues worthy of wider debate and policy discussion, but also of a much fuller appreciation by professionals in the criminal justice and medical fields of one another's current principles and practice. Such a need was also apparent within the criminal justice field itself.

The research study also indicated the need for establishing clearly stated routines, for co-operation and sharing of information. Information gaps occurred between police and courts, between courts and hospitals, and between courts and prisons. More important gaps occurred between police and courts in the clarity of the reports returned to them. It is suggested that the specific questions asked and answered in some areas should be made explicit everywhere. The implicit acceptance of what is thought to be wanted, why and when, leads to delays and misunderstandings.

On the question of the type of case where advice should be sought, there seemed to be general agreement within the criminal justice system. Although some suggested that it would be helpful to have guidelines to typify those alleged offenders on whom psychiatric advice was necessary, it seems likely that any set of rules wide enough to encompass all needs would result in an avalanche of requests for reports. The two pointers of behaviour and history appear to be generally recommended in principle by writers and found in practice by researchers.

One result of the awareness of the possibility of mental disorder that may not be fully appreciated is that it leads to an emphasis on individual decisions in individual circumstances. Some doctors stressed the necessity for this and felt there were dangers in too formalised a system. On the other hand, decisions at present may depend to an unacceptable degree on attitudes towards offenders and offending of individual policemen, prosecutors, psychiatrists and sentencers, and on the degree of communication between them.[5]

However, it should also be remembered that, although psychiatrists cannot offer treatment to all the personality-disordered, the petty recidivists or the alcoholics, the sex offenders or the fire-raisers, there is no suggestion that these persons should not therefore be examined. If advice is sought, the responsibility of diagnosis still rests with the psychiatrist, who is thus lifting some of the burden of responsibility from the shoulders of the decision-makers in the criminal justice system.

What is important is that this burden of responsibility differs according to the decision-maker's position. The police—as laymen, as members of the public—have a personal responsibility, whereas procurators fiscal and sheriffs have a professional one. And there is a further difference in that the psychiatrist, because he has the opportunity of selecting those whom he can treat, is able to limit his own responsibility. Such a freedom of choice is not available to the police or courts, with whom remains the responsibility of deciding upon the steps to be taken with those for whom psychiatric treatment is not appropriate—the responsibility for the decisions involved in detaining, prosecuting and sentencing.

In Scotland the group of offenders who may be mentally abnormal appears to be a very small one in relation to the whole population arrested or coming within the criminal justice system, and so must be kept in perspective in relation to the question of allocating resources, but at the same time it is not without influence in any consideration of the aims of the criminal justice system itself. Where this group of persons is concerned, the system may be uneasily attempting to combine the protection of society and the provision of medical treatment for offenders with the upholding of justice.

2   Wider issues relating to the control of crime and mental abnormality

Whilst this study has focused on the role of the public prosecutor in dealing with the apparently mentally disturbed offender, it is fully recognised that the issues relating to prosecution are part of an interrelated network of other facets of the law enforcement and criminal justice processes: the police, the courts, the prisons and community-based penal measures. They are related also to other forms of social control as indicated in Chapter 1. Alternative forms of social control may be of a formal or informal nature and of particular importance in the present context is the ready availability of medical services. Currently there is much debate and concern on the one hand as to the philosophical foundations of the criminal justice processes and on the other hand as to the nature and content of psychiatric treatment. One will only be able to look to the future with some degree of specificity after those fundamental issues have been resolved.

As regards criminal justice, in countries in the Western World penal policy continues to be under intensive review 'in the light of the extensive collapse of the "rehabilitative ideal" which had improved much of post-war penal thought'.[6] This collapse is related to the re-examination of the roles of the police and of prosecution services as 'the gate-keepers' of the criminal justice system, especially in relation to their special powers, the exercise of discretion, and their accountability both locally and nationally. It is of considerable significance that at the present juncture it has been decided to introduce a public prosecution system in England, so that many of the issues relating to the Scottish system, as well as public prosecution systems elsewhere, can be of particular relevance to the way in which the new English system develops.

In looking to the future in relation to the possible ways in which criminal justice processes may be improved, two points need to be stressed. Firstly, 'criminal justice will never be anything but an unpleasant social necessity:

there is no way to accomplish it joyfully';[7] and secondly, that 'where researchers and policy-makers have undertaken a critical examination of the structure of their criminal justice systems, they have found that there are few common aims, that there is considerable diffusion of duties and responsibilities and little or no co-ordination between the sub-systems, and that there are often differing views regarding the role of each part of the system'.[8]

If the present institutional arrangements for dealing with crime continue, then it is clear that the issues relating to discretion and accountability of police and prosecution decision-making will become of even greater significance than at present. Recent trends in most Western criminal justice systems have led to more and more criminal cases being settled outside the formal system of criminal justice,[9] with the consequent problems of low visibility of decision-making and a lack of formal processes of public accountability. This is in vivid contrast to the articulated structured discretion and precise forms of public review with respect to those cases that come into the formal criminal justice process. The present ways of dealing with the issues of apparent mental abnormality at the early stages of law-enforcement amply illustrate that phenomenon. Current thinking, however, tends to maintain the grand rhetoric about criminal justice, yet at the same time advocates that a greater proportion of cases be excluded from the criminal justice process by 'the gate-keepers', while on the important question of accountability little more than some form of guideline is being proposed. More radical alternatives to this trend have been suggested including that of 'the minimalist response'.[10] A different kind of radical alternative is put forward by Lloyd Weinreb of Harvard University, which involves the restructuring of the institutions relating to police, prosecution and the preliminary investigation of crime. He provocatively proposes that (1) the investigative responsibility of the police, except in so far as it is an incidental aspect of their peace-keeping and emergency functions, be reassigned to an independent branch of the judiciary and (2) primary responsibility for investigating a crime, preparing an accusation and proving guilt be joined in a single agency.[11] The point to stress here is that the institutions relating to crime control have undergone considerable modifications and development over the years, and there is no reason to suppose that that process will not continue in the future. This means that, while it is important to consider the problems of dealing with the apparently mentally abnormal offender within the existing criminal justice system, it is also important to see how these issues might be dealt with in a radically different approach to the criminal justice processes. In the area of mental health, also, there have been very substantial and fundamental changes in recent years with respect to both theoretical issues and the practical arrangements for dealing with patients. Again, these kinds of developments are likely to continue into the future and could therefore significantly alter the context in which issues relating to the mentally abnormal offender are considered, especially those relating to custodial control and of control without custody.[12]

Three important areas relating to decision-making with respect to apparently mentally abnormal offenders are: dangerousness and criminality; alcohol- and drug-related offences; and the socially inadequate offender. Each of these has a direct bearing on the interface between criminal justice and psychiatry both at the conceptual or theoretical level and at the practical level. In the past the criminal justice personnel have tended to rely on the expert opinion of the psychiatrist in relation to the diagnosis of 'dangerousness' and its practical implications for the protection of the public. Recent studies, however, have indicated that 'dangerousness' is not particularly related to those offenders whom psychiatrists diagnose as mentally abnormal. Furthermore, the concept of 'dangerousness' is not primarily a psychiatric one but includes ethical, legal and political criteria so that the decision whether or not to detain on grounds of dangerousness at the early stages of criminal justice, cannot be based primarily on medical opinion.[13] The debate continues. The issues of the relationship of crime to alcohol and drugs have a long history both in public and legal debate and in research. It is generally accepted today that they are related; but the nature of that relationship remains unsettled especially in the sphere of mental health. The question of how to deal with issues relating to such offenders is still very much under-researched, but the practical question of obtaining advice as to apparent mental disorder in relation to alcohol and drug offenders remains primarily a question of resources available, both as regards diagnostic work and facilities for medical treatment. Finally, the concept of the 'socially inadequate offender' raises the issue as to whether 'socially inadequate' can be regarded as a condition that can be properly ascertained psychiatricly or whether it is primarily a description of those who are unable to cope within a particular social environment. Where this description is related to petty criminality it indicates 'the unwanted offender', unwanted by both the medical and penal services. Without additional kinds of facilities for dealing with such offenders there is rarely much practical value in obtaining medical reports on them at the early stages of the criminal justice processes. Such offenders tend to form a growing proportion of the daily prison population.

It is hoped that this study of the issues of prosecution in relation to the apparently mentally disturbed offender will facilitate communication among those concerned in making decisions and that it will promote public discussion of matters of practice and public policy in dealing with such offenders.

Appendix I

Relevant Legislation

A: Scotland

The Mental Health (Scotland) Act 1960 and the Criminal Procedure (Scotland) Act 1975 were in force at the time of the research project and at the time of writing. The relevant Sections are noted below.

The Mental Health (Amendment) (Scotland) Act 1983 will become effective late in 1984. It makes provision for interim hospital orders and for a right of appeal by patients subject to restriction orders, but other changes are of a minor nature as far as criminal proceedings are concerned.

From *Mental Health (Scotland) Act 1960:*

Definition of mental disorder

6. In this Act "mental disorder" means mental illness or mental deficiency however caused or manifested.

Patients liable to be detained in hospital or subject to guardianship.

23.—(1) A person who is suffering from any mental disorder that requires or is susceptible to medical treatment may be admitted to a hospital or received into guardianship in pursuance of the appropriate application under the following provisions of this Act; but, without prejudice to the said provisions so far as relating to emergency admission, no person over the age of twenty-one years shall be so admitted or received except where the mental disorder from which he suffers—

(*a*) is mental deficiency such that he is incapable of living an independent life or of guarding himself against serious exploitation; or

(*b*) is a mental illness other than a persistent disorder which is manifested only by abnormally aggressive or seriously irresponsible conduct.

From *Criminal Procedure (Scotland) Act 1975:*

Power of court to commit to hospital a person suffering from mental disorder.

25.—(1) Where a court remands or commits for trial a person charged with any offence who appears to the court to be suffering from mental disorder, and the court is satisfied that a hospital is available for his admission and suitable for his detention, the court may, instead of remanding him in custody, commit him to that hospital.

1960 c. 61.

(2) Where any person is committed to a hospital as aforesaid, the hospital shall be specified in the warrant and, if the responsible medical officer is satisfied that he is suffering from mental disorder of a nature or degree which warrants his admission to a hospital under Part IV of the Mental Health (Scotland) Act 1960, he shall there be detained for the period for which he is remanded or the period of committal, unless before the expiration of that period he is liberated in due course of law.

(3) When the responsible medical officer has examined the person so detained he shall report the result of that examination to the court and, where the report is to the effect that the person is not suffering from mental disorder of such a nature or degree as aforesaid, the court may commit him to any

prison or other institution to which he might have been committed had he not been committed to hospital or may otherwise deal with him according to law.

(4) No person shall be committed to a hospital under this section except on the written or oral evidence of a medical practitioner.

Procedure at trial of persons suffering from mental disorder

Insanity in bar of trial or as the ground of acquittal.

174.—(1) Where any person charged on indictment with the commission of an offence is found insane so that the trial of that person upon the indictment cannot proceed, or if in the course of the trial of any person so indicted it appears to the jury that he is insane, the court shall direct a finding to that effect to be recorded.

(2) Where in the case of any person charged as aforesaid evidence is brought before the court that that person was insane at the time of doing the act or making the omission constituting the offence with which he is charged and the person is acquitted, the court shall direct the jury to find whether the person was insane at such time as aforesaid, and to declare whether the person was acquitted by them on account of his insanity at that time

(3) Where the court has directed that a finding be recorded in pursuance of subsection (1) of this section, or where a jury has declared that a person has been acquitted by them on the ground of his insanity in pursuance of the last foregoing subsection, the court shall order that the person to whom that finding or that acquittal relates shall be detained in a State hospital or such other hospital as for special reasons the court may specify.

(4) An order for the detention of a person in a hospital under this section shall have the like effect as a hospital order (within the meaning of section 175(3) of this Act) together with an order restricting his discharge made without limitation of time; and where such an order is given in respect of a person while he is in the hospital, he shall be deemed to be admitted in pursuance of, and on the date of the order.

(5) Where it appears to a court that it is not practicable or appropriate for the accused to be brought before it for the purpose of determining whether he is insane so that his trial cannot proceed, then, if no objection to such a course is taken by or on behalf of the accused, the court may order that the case be proceeded with in his absence.

Power of court to order hospital admission or guardianship.

175.—(1) Where a person is convicted in the High Court or the sheriff court of an offence, other than an offence the sentence for which is fixed by law, punishable by that court with imprisonment, and the following conditions are satisfied, that is to say—

(a) the court is satisfied, on the written or oral evidence of two medical practitioners (complying with the provisions of section 176 of this Act) that the offender is suffering from mental disorder of a nature or degree which, in the case of a person under 21 years of age, would warrant his admission to a hospital or his reception into guardianship

1960 c. 61.

under Part IV of the Mental Health (Scotland) Act 1960, and

(b) the court is of opinion, having regard to all the circumstances including the nature of the offence and the character and antecedents of the offender, and to the other available methods of dealing with him, that the most suitable method of disposing of the case is by means of an order under this section,

the court may by order authorise his admission to and detention in such hsopital as may be specified in the order or, as the case may be, place him under the guardianship of such local authority or of such other person approved by a local authority as may be so specified:

Provided that, where his case is remitted by the sheriff to the High Court for sentence under any enactment, the power to make an order under this subsection shall be exercisable by that court.

(2) Where it appears to the prosecutor in any court before which a person is charged with an offence that the person may be suffering from mental disorder, it shall be the duty of such prosecutor to bring before the court such evidence as may be available of the mental condition of that person.

(3) An order for the admission of a person to a hospital (in this Act, referred to as "a hospital order") shall not be made under this section in respect of an offender unless the court is satisfied that that hospital, in the event of such an order being made by the court, is available for his admission thereto within 28 days of the making of such an order.

(4) A State hospital shall not be specified in a hospital order in respect of the detention of a person unless the court is satisfied, on the evidence of the medical practitioners which is taken into account under paragraph (a) of subsection (1) of this section, that the offender, on account of his dangerous, violent or criminal propensities, requires treatment under conditions of special security, and cannot suitably be cared for in a hospital other than a State hospital.

(5) An order placing a person under the guardianship of a local authority or of any other person (in this Act referred to as "a guardianship order") shall not be made under this section unless the court is satisfied that the authority or person is willing to receive that person into guardianship.

(6) A hospital order or guardianship order shall specify the form of mental disorder, being mental illness or mental deficiency or both, from which, upon the evidence taken into account under paragraph (a) of subsection (1) of this section, the offender is found by the court to be suffering; and no such order shall be made unless the offender is described by each of the practitioners, whose evidence is taken into account as aforesaid, as suffering from the same form of mental disorder, whether or not he is also described by either of them as suffering from the other form.

(7) Where an order is made under this section, the court shall not pass sentence of imprisonment or impose a fine or make a probation order in respect of the offence, but may make any other order which the court has power to make apart from this section; and for the purposes of this subsection "sentence of imprisonment" includes any sentence or order for detention.

Requirements as to medical evidence.

1960 c. 61.

176.—(1) of the medical practitioners whose evidence is taken into account under section 175(1)(a) of this Act, at least one shall be a practitioner approved for the purposes of section 27 of the Mental Health (Scotland) Act 1960 by a Health Board as having special experience in the diagnosis or treatment of mental disorder.

(2) For the purposes of the said section 175(1)(a) a report in writing purporting to be signed by a medical practitioner may, subject to the provisions of this section, be received in evidence without proof of the signature or qualifications of the practitioner; but the court may, in any case, require that the practitioner by whom such a report was signed be called to give oral evidence.

(3) Where any such report as aforesaid is tendered in evidence, otherwise than by or on behalf of the accused, then—

(a) if the accused is represented by counsel or solicitor, a copy of the report shall be given to his counsel or solicitor;

(b) if the accused is not so represented, the substance of the report shall be disclosed to the accused or, where he is a child under 16 years of age, to his parent or guardian if present in court;

(c) in any case, the accused may require that the practitioner by whom the report was signed be called to give oral evidence, and evidence to rebut the evidence contained in the report may be called by or on behalf of the accused;

and where the court is of opinion that further time is necessary in the interests of the accused for consideration of that report, or the substance of any such report, it shall adjourn the case.

(4) For the purpose of calling evidence to rebut the evidence contained in any such report as aforesaid, arrangements may be made by or on behalf of an accused person detained in a hospital for his examination by any medical practitioner, and any such examination may be made in private.

Supplementary provisions as to hospital orders.

1968 c. 49.

177. The court by which a hospital order is made may give such directions as it thinks fit for the conveyance of the patient to a place of safety and his detention therein pending his admission to the hospital within the period of 28 days referred to in section 175(3) of this Act; but a direction for the conveyance of a patient to a residential establishment provided by a local authority under Part IV of the Social Work (Scotland) Act 1968 shall not be given unless the court is satisfied that that authority is willing to receive the patient therein.

Power of court to restrict discharge from hospital.

1960 c. 61.

178.—(1) Where a hospital order is made in respect of a person, and it appears to the court, having regard to the nature of the offence with which he is charged, the antecedents of the person and the risk that as a result of his mental disorder he would commit offences if set at large, that it is necessary for the protection of the public so to do, the court, may, subject to the provisions of this section, further order that the person shall be subject to the special restrictions set out in section 60(3) of the Mental Health (Scotland) Act 1960, either without limit of time or during such period as may be specified in the order.

(2) An order under this section (in this Act referred to as "an order restricting discharge") shall not be made in the case of any person unless the medical practitioner approved by the Health Board for the purposes of section 27 of the Mental Health (Scotland) Act 1960, whose evidence is taken into account by the court under section 175(1)(a) of this Act, has given evidence orally before the court.

(3) Where an order restricting the discharge of a patient is in force, a guardianship order shall not be made in respect of him; and where the hospital order relating to him ceases to have effect by virtue of section 58(4) of the Mental Health (Scotland) Act 1960 on the making of another hospital order, that order shall have the same effect in relation to the order restricting discharge as the previous hospital order, but without prejudice to the power of the court making that other hospital order to make another order restricting discharge to have effect on the expiration of the previous such order.

These provisions of the Criminal Procedure (Scotland) Act 1975 relate to prosecution on indictment and they are replicated in Sections 330, 375, 377, 378 and 379 for summary procedure (i.e. in respect of less serious offences)

B: England and Wales

At the time of the research the Mental Health Act 1959 was in force. This has now been superseded by the Mental Health Act 1983. Textual references and the excerpts which follow are taken from the 1983 Act.

Application of Act: "mental disorder".

1.—(1) The provisions of this Act shall have effect with respect to the reception, care and treatment of mentally disordered patients, the management of their property and other related matters.

(2) In this Act—

"mental disorder" means mental illness, arrested or incomplete development of mind, psychopathic disorder and any other disorder or disability of mind and "mentally disordered" shall be construed accordingly;

"severe mental impairment" means a state of arrested or incomplete development of mind which includes severe impairment of intelligence and social functioning and is associated with abnormally aggressive or seriously irresponsible conduct on the part of the person concerned and "severely mentally impaired" shall be construed accordingly;

"mental impairment" means a state of arrested or incomplete development of mind (not amounting to severe mental impairment) which includes significant impairment of intelligence and social functioning and is associated with abnormally aggressive or seriously irresponsible conduct on the part of the person concerned and "mentally impaired" shall be construed accordingly;

"psychopathic disorder" means a persistent disorder or disability of mind (whether or not including significant impairment of intelligence) which results in abnormally aggressive or seriously irresponsible conduct on the part of the person concerned;

and other expressions shall have the meanings assigned to them in section 145 below.

(3) Nothing in subsection (2) above shall be construed as implying that a person may be dealt with under this Act as suffering from mental disorder, or from any form of mental disorder described in this section, by reason only of promiscuity or other immoral conduct, sexual deviancy or dependence on alcohol or drugs.

Remand to hospital for report on accused's mental condition.

35.—(1) Subject to the provisions of this section, the Crown Court or a magistrates' court may remand an accused person to a hospital specified by the court for a report on his mental condition.

(2) For the purposes of this section an accused person is—

(a) in relation to the Crown Court, any person who is awaiting trial before the court for an offence punishable with imprisonment or who has been arraigned before the court for such an offence and has not yet been sentenced or otherwise dealt with for the offence on which he has been arraigned;

(b) in relation to a magistrates' court, any person who has been convicted by the court of an offence punishable on summary conviction with imprisonment and any person charged with such an offence if the court is satisfied that he did the act or made the omission charged or he has consented to the exercise by the court of the powers conferred by this section.

(3) Subject to subsection (4) below, the powers conferred by this section may be exercised if—

    (*a*) the court is satisfied, on the written or oral evidence of a registered medical practitioner, that there is reason to suspect that the accused person is suffering from mental illness, psychopathic disorder, severe mental impairment or mental impairment; and

    (*b*) the court is of the opinion that it would be impracticable for a report on his mental condition to be made if he were remanded on bail;

but those powers shall not be exercised by the Crown Court in respect of a person who has been convicted before the court if the sentence for the offence of which he has been convicted is fixed by law.

(4) The court shall not remand an accused person to a hospital under this section unless satisfied, on the written or oral evidence of the registered medical practitioner who would be responsible for making the report or of some other person representing the managers of the hospital, that arrangements have been made for his admission to that hospital and for his admission to it within the period of seven days beginning with the date of the remand; and if the court is so satisfied it may, pending his admission, give directions for his conveyance to and detention in a place of safety.

Remand of accused person to hospital for treatment.   **36.**—(1) Subject to the provisions of this section, the Crown Court may, instead of remanding an accused person in custody, remand him to a hospital specified by the court if satisfied, on the written or oral evidence of two registered medical practitioners, that he is suffering from mental illness or severe mental impairment of a nature or degree which makes it appropriate for him to be detained in a hospital for medical treatment.

(2) For the purposes of this section an accused person is any person who is in custody awaiting trial before the Crown Court for an offence punishable with imprisonment (other than an offence the sentence for which is fixed by law) or who at any time before sentence is in custody in the course of a trial before that court for such an offence.

(3) The court shall not remand an accused person under this section to a hospital unless it is satisfied, on the written or oral evidence of the registered medical practitioner who would be in charge of his treatment or of some other person representing the managers of the hospital, that arrangements have been made for his admission to that hospital and for his admission to it within the period of seven days beginning with the date of the remand; and if the court is so satisfied it may, pending his admission, give direction for his conveyance to and detention in a place of safety.

Powers of courts to order hospital admission or guardianship.   **37.**—(1) Where a person is convicted before the Crown Court of an offence punishable with imprisonment other than an offence the sentence for which is fixed by law, or is convicted by a magistrates' court of an offence punishable on summary conviction with imprisonment, and the conditions mentioned in subsection (2) below are satisfied, the court may by order authorise his admission to and detention in such hospital as may be specified in the order or, as the case may be, place him under the guardianship of a local social services authority as may be so specified.

(2) The conditions referred to in subsection (1) above are that—

    (*a*) the court is satisfied, on the written or oral evidence of two registered medical practitioners, that the offender is suffering from mental illness, psychopathic disorder, severe mental impairment or mental impairment and that either—

        (i) the mental disorder from which the offender is suffering is of a nature or degree which makes it appropriate for him to be detained in a hospital for medical treatment and, in the case of psychopathic disorder or mental impairment, that such treatment is likely to alleviate or prevent a deterioration of his condition; or

(ii) in the case of an offender who has attained the age of 16 years, the mental disorder is of a nature or degree which warrants his reception into guardianship under this Act; and

(*b*) the court is of the opinion, having regard to all the circumstances including the nature of the offence and the character and antecedents of the offender, and to the other available methods of dealing with him, that the most suitable method of disposing of the case is by means of an order under this section.

(3) Where a person is charged before a magistrates' court with any act or omission as an offence and the court would have power, on convicting him of that offence, to make an order under subsection (1) above in his case as being a person suffering from mental illness or severe mental impairment, then if the court is satisfied that the accused did the act or made the omission charged, the court may, if it thinks fit, make such an order without convicting him.

(4) An order for the admission of an offender to a hospital (in this Act referred to as "a hospital order") shall not be made under this section unless the court is satisfied on the written or oral evidence of the registered medical practitioner who would be in charge of his treatment or of some other person representing the managers of the hospital that arrangements have been made for his admission to that hospital in the event of such an order being made by the court, and for his admission to it within the period of 28 days beginning with the date of the making of such an order; and the court may, pending his admission within that period, give such directions as it thinks fit for his conveyance to and detention in a place of safety.

Interim hospital orders. **38.**—(1) Where a person is convicted before the Crown Court of an offence punishable with imprisonment (other than an offence the sentence for which is fixed by law) or is convicted by a magistrates' court of an offence punishable on summary conviction with imprisonment and the court before or by which he is convicted is satisfied, on the written or oral evidence of two registered medical practitioners—

(*a*) that the offender is suffering from mental illness, psychopathic disorder, severe mental impairment or mental impairment; and

(*b*) that there is reason to suppose that the mental disorder from which the offender is suffering is such that it may be appropriate for a hospital order to be made in his case,

the court may, before making a hospital order or dealing with him in some other way, make an order (in this Act referred to as "an interim hospital order") authorising his admission to such hospital as may be specified in the order and his detention there in accordance with this section.

(2) In the case of an offender who is subject to an interim hospital order the court may make a hospital order without his being brought before the court if he is represented by counsel or a solicitor and his counsel or solicitor is given an opportunity of being heard.

(3) At least one of the registered medical practitioners whose evidence is taken into account under subsection (1) above shall be employed at the hospital which is to be specified in the order.

(4) An interim hospital order shall not be made for the admission of an offender to a hospital unless the court is satisfied, on the written or oral evidence of the registered medical practitioner who would be in charge of his treatment or of some other person representing the managers of the hospital,

that arrangements have been made for his admission to that hospital and for his admission to it within the period of 28 days beginning wtih the date of the order; and if the court is so satisfied the court may, pending his admission, give directions for his convcyance to and detention in a place of safety.

Power of higher courts to restrict discharge from hospital.

41.—(1) Where a hospital order is made in respect of an offender by the Crown Court, and it appears to the court, having regard to the nature of the offence, the antecedents of the offender and the risk of his committing further offences if set at large, that it is necessary for the protection of the public from serious harm so to do, the court may, subject to the provisions of this section, further order that the offender shall be subject to the special restrictions set out in this section, either without limit of time or during such period as may be specified in the order; and an order under this section shall be known as "a restriction order".

(2) A restriction order shall not be made in the case of any person unless at least one of the registered medical practitioners whose evidence is taken into account by the court under section 37(2)(a) above has given evidence orally before the court.

Powers of Secretary of State in respect of patients subject to restriction orders.

42.—(1) If the Secretary of State is satisfied that in the case of any patient a restriction order is no longer required for the protection of the public from serious harm, he may direct that the patient shall cease to be subject to the special restrictions set out in section 41(3) above; and where the Secretary of State so directs, the restriction order shall cease to have effect, and section 41(5) above shall apply accordingly.

(2) At any time while a restriction order is in force in respect of a patient, the Secretary of State may, if he thinks fit, by warrant discharge the patient from hospital, either absolutely or subject to conditions; and where a person is absolutely discharged under this subsection, he shall thereupon cease to be liable to be detained by virtue of the relevant hospital order, and the restriction order shall cease to have effect accordingly.

(3) The Secretary of State may at any time during the continuance in force of a restriction order in respect of a patient who has been conditionally discharged under subsection (2) above by warrant recall the patient to such hospital as may be specified in the warrant.

Power of magistrates' courts to commit for restriction order.

43.—(1) If in the case of a person of or over the age of 14 years who is convicted by a magistrates' court of an offence punishable on summary conviction with imprisonment—

(a) the conditions which under section 37(1) above are required to be satisfied for the making of a hospital order are satisfied in respect of the offender; but

(b) it appears to the court, having regard to the nature of the offence, the antecedents of the offender and the risk of his committing further offences if set at large, that if a hospital order is made a restriction order should also be made,

the court may, instead of making a hospital order or dealing with him in any other manner, commit him in custody to the Crown Court to be dealt with in respect of the offence.

(2) Where an offender is committed to the Crown Court under this section, the Crown Court shall inquire into the circumstances of the case and may—

(a) if that court would have power so to do under the foregoing provisions of this Part of this Act upon the conviction of the offender before that court of such an offence as is described in section 37(1) above, make a hospital order in his case, with or without a restriction order;

(b) if the court does not make such an order, deal with the offender in any other manner in which the magistrates' court might have dealt with him.

Applications to tribunals concerning restricted patients.

70.—A patient who is a restricted patient within the meaning of section 79 below and is detained in a hospital may apply to a Mental Health Review Tribunal—

(a) in the period between the expiration of six months and the expiration of 12 months beginning with the date of the relevant hospital order or transfer direction; and

(b) in any subsequent period of 12 months.

Interpretation of Part V.

79.—(1) In this Part of this Act "restricted patient" means a patient who is subject to a restriction order or restriction direction and this Part of this Act shall, subject to the provisions of this section, have effect in relation to any person who—

(a) is subject to a direction which by virtue of section 46(3) above has the same effect as a hospital order and a restriction order; or

1964 c. 84.
1968 c. 19.

(b) is treated as subject to a hospital order and a restriction order by virtue of an order under section 5(1) of the Criminal Procedure (Insanity) Act 1964 or section 6 or 14(1) of the Criminal Appeal Act 1968; or

1960 c. 61.

(c) is treated as subject to a hospital order and a restriction order or to a transfer direction and a restriction direction by virtue of section 82(2) or 85(2) below or section 73(2) of the Mental Health (Scotland) Act 1960,

as it has effect in relation to a restricted patient.

Appendix II

Scottish Research

Details of the research: the size of the problem of mental abnormality in arrest and prosecution, and the composition of the sample

In order to build up a register of requests for medical reports relating to the mental state of alleged offenders during the year 1979 every police force and every procurator fiscal and/or sheriff clerk was asked to send a quarterly list of names (and reference number where appropriate).

Police forces in some areas documented the 'grey' area where an incident or individual was handled without the necessity of a formal charge. The figures given refer, so far as can be ascertained, to persons charged, but some areas may not have differentiated between their cases, and there could be a slight overestimate.

As noted in Chapters 4 and 5, in some areas procurators fiscal arrange for all psychiatric reports to be made, whether ordered by them before plea or at the request of the court before sentence. Some sheriff clerks confirmed that this was their practice and that all relevant names would therefore appear on procurator fiscal lists. In other areas sheriff clerks arrange their own pre-sentence reports. Possible results of these practices are an artificial inflation of procurator fiscal figures and a reduction in sheriff clerk figures, and also possible duplication where both procurator fiscal and sheriff clerk sent lists of the same names. However, since names rather than total numbers were requested, it proved possible to check on individuals appearing in more than one place or more than one service. As with any exercise which counts, at one specific period, differing stages of an ongoing process (and in the criminal justice system the process can be one of many months) totals are not reconcilable because of the time lag in that process.

Table 1, therefore, summarises total numbers of individuals—by sex, by service and by area—for whom psychiatric reports were requested in 1979, followed by a note of the overlap.

Overlap

One hundred and one of the 404 persons named by the *police* appeared again in either procurator fiscal or sheriff clerk lists, or indeed in both. This is to be expected if the police role is that of alerting the courts to possible problems. As procurators fiscal and sheriff clerks would arrange for their own psychiatric reports in addition to any police report, it is reasonable to count both requests.

If procurator fiscal and sheriff clerk numbers are taken together to give some indication of total *court* requests, then there is an overlap of some 206 persons appearing in both lists. This is a consequence of the duplication referred to above (arising particularly in Edinburgh, Perth, Falkirk, Aberdeen and Elgin) and, as the same requests for reports are being counted twice, the figure should be deducted from the court total of 1585 giving a figure of 1379 requests for reports from the courts. These are detailed by area in Table 2.

The total may well be an underestimate because of one unforeseeable problem in relation to 1979 figures, namely that sheriff clerk figures are artificially low for the first half of the year because of industrial action by court staff and despite the rise in the second half of the year, the yearly total may be artificially low. There are no general comparative figures for other years but some areas had information: Aberdeen and Glasgow show respectively 10% and 14% decreases, Hamilton a 30% decrease and Airdrie a decrease on reported figures of almost 60%. The Scottish Health Services Council report on *Forensic Psychiatry* in October 1968, referred to 1964 and to an estimated 1700 reports per annum, a figure which included all reports (i.e. juveniles were included) and gave a rate of 33 reports per 100,000 of the population. If the 1979 figures for adults only are related to the population aged 17 and over, the rate is 43 per 100,000 which is a considerable increase over the decade. The 1968 report also referred to wide *area variations* and a similar position obtained in 1979. Table 3 relates police requests and court requests (i.e. totalling figures and allowing for overlap) in 1979 to population figures and to published crime figures by *police area* from *Criminal Statistics (Scotland) 1978*.

Sampling

The register established, in statistical terms, a population on which a sample could be based. The scope of the research did not permit a detailed examination of all cases, which would in any event have meant unwarranted demands on time and resources of already busy offices. It was therefore decided to attempt to obtain information on a 1 in 4 basis from each area of each service, selecting cases by putting names into alphabetical order and taking every fourth case (or one where less than 4 were concerned). Some cases could not be traced and some cases could not be included because they were not yet complete. In these instances others were substituted where possible. The composition of the sample in relation to total numbers reported is as shown in Table 4.

The two facets of the research, empirical data collection and discussions with officials, continued simultaneously throughout the research period, and it was from these early discussions that a questionnaire was developed (see page 121) for use in connection with the sample. Data were collected in two stages relating to January–June and July–December of 1979. Forms giving names and reference numbers were sent to police, to procurators fiscal and to sheriff clerks and the response was almost 100 per cent. One procurator fiscal on principle did not wish to divulge information on individual cases, and one psychiatrist did not wish to give individual reports, but these only involved five cases. Other gaps or problems arose from administrative concerns such as illness.

In the event there proved to be considerable variations in the quantity and quality of information collected. Because the project was adding yet another burden to already busy offices, it was apparent that some latitude had to be given in regard to the manner and timing of the return of questionnaires, but, in addition to this, very great differences became apparent in the routine operations of the many people involved. Each police force is independent, each procurator fiscal is independent, each sheriff court is independent in its record-keeping, and information readily available in one instance was inaccessible or indeed non-existent in another.

Police forces and sheriff clerks' offices in the main returned completed questionnaires. Some procurator fiscal offices returned incomplete questionnaires and summarised the account of the incident giving rise to police charges, previous convictions and the content of psychiatric reports. Within these the amount of detail varied considerably. The more general pattern was for a questionnaire to be returned from procurators fiscal along with photocopies of police reports or of previous convictions or of psychiatric reports—or indeed with all of these. Some fiscal offices sent us original papers, but these varied from a small selection chosen as important by the office concerned, to vast boxes containing all the precognitions in a complicated murder trial (which were returned to the offices concerned on completion of the project). Even in these cases, however, there was a lack of uniformity from a research viewpoint which not only resulted in some gaps in data, but also led to an awareness of gaps in the questions asked and information sought. We do not seek to use this as an excuse for our own omissions, but are rather very grateful to all those who co-operated so willingly and who made us aware of possible shortcomings in our data.

TABLE 1.

No. of persons for whom psychiatric reports sought by service and by area in 1979

POLICE				PROCURATOR FISCAL (Regional offices)				SHERIFF CLERK (PF = numbers included in P.F. figures)			
	M.	F.	T.		M.	F.	T.		M.	F.	T.
STRATHCLYDE	124	59	183	**GLASGOW & STRATHKELVIN**							
				Glasgow	108	10	118	Glasgow	101	9	110
				NORTH STRATHCLYDE							
				Campbeltown	5	—	5	Campbeltown	2	—	2
				Dumbarton	37	9	46	Dumbarton (PF)	—	—	—
				Dunoon	—	1	1	Dunoon	4	2	6
				Greenock	7	—	7	Greenock (PF)	—	—	—
				Kilmarnock	21	4	25	Kilmarnock	14	—	14
				Oban	2	1	3				
				Paisley	27	5	32	Paisley	—	—	—
				Rothesay	4	—	4				
				Sub-total	103	20	123	Sub-total	20	2	22
				SOUTH STRATHCLYDE DUMFRIES & GALLOWAY							
				Airdrie	15	2	17	Airdrie	52	8	60
				Ayr	15	7	22	Ayr	6	2	8
				Hamilton	35	10	45	Hamilton	39	11	50
				Lanark	2	—	2	Lanark	2	—	2
				Dumfries	18	3	21	Dumfries	17	3	20
DUMFRIES & GALLOWAY	16	5	21	Kirkcudbright	—	—	—	Kirkcudbright	—	—	—
				Stranraer	9	1	10	Stranraer (PF)	—	—	—
				Sub-total	94	23	117	Sub-total	116	24	140

TABLE 1 *contd.*

LOTHIAN & BORDERS — region totals: 73, 36, 109

Town				Town			
Edinburgh	46	21	67	Edinburgh	78	22	100
Duns	1	1	2	Duns	10	—	10
Haddington	2	—	2	Haddington	8	—	8
Jedburgh	—	—	—	Jedburgh	11	3	14
Linlithgow	23	2	25	Linlithgow	—	—	—
Peebles	—	—	—				
Selkirk	7	1	8	Selkirk	6	—	6
Sub-total	79	25	104	Sub-total	113	25	138

TAYSIDE, CENTRAL AND FIFE

TAYSIDE — region totals: 13, 13, 24
CENTRAL — region totals: 2, —, 2
FIFE — region totals: 8, 2, 10

Town				Town			
Dundee	57	8	65	Dundee (PF)	—	—	36
Arbroath	8	1	9	Arbroath	31	5	36
Forfar	36	4	40	Forfar (PF)	—	—	24
Perth	23	6	29	Perth	22	2	24
Alloa	—	—	—	Alloa	11	2	13
Stirling	8	—	8	Stirling	15	3	18
Falkirk	14	2	16	Falkirk	12	5	17
Cupar	11	3	14	Cupar (PF)	—	—	21
Dunfermline	—	—	—	Dunfermline	17	4	21
Kirkcaldy	12	2	14	Kirkcaldy	19	7	26
Sub-total	169	26	195	Sub-total	127	28	155

TABLE 1 *contd.*

GRAMPIAN, HIGHLANDS AND ISLANDS

Region			
GRAMPIAN	31	9	40
NORTHERN	13	2	15
TOTALS	280	124	404

Place				Place			
Aberdeen	99	30	129	Aberdeen	84	19	103
Banff	9	—	9	Banff (PF)	3	3	6
Elgin	17	5	22	Elgin	—	—	—
Peterhead	—	—	—	Peterhead	—	—	—
Stonehaven	1	1	2	Stonehaven (PF)	—	—	—
Dingwall	8	—	8	Dingwall	3	5	8
Dornoch	1	—	1	Dornoch	—	—	—
Inverness	6	1	7	Inverness	28	11	39
Fort William	2	—	2	Fort William	2	1	3
Lochmaddy	—	—	—				
Portree	—	—	—				
Stornoway	6	1	7				
Kirkwall	1	—	1	Kirkwall (PF)	—	—	—
Lerwick	—	—	—	Lerwick	—	—	—
Tain	—	—	—				
Wick	9	7	16	Wick (PF)	—	—	—
Sub-total	159	45	204	Sub-total	120	39	159
TOTALS	712	149	861	TOTALS	597	127	724
GRAND TOTAL	1589	400	1989				

Reports were requested on a second occasion on 13 persons — 11 persons — 8 persons giving a total of 2021 reports

TABLE 2

Total numbers of persons for whom psychiatric reports requested by courts in 1979 (based on returns from procurators fiscal and sheriff clerks and allowing for overlap between them) and totals for police areas

COURT		Sub-total by P.F. Regions	Police area	Overall total for police area
Glasgow & Strathkelvin				
Glasgow	220	220		
North Strathclyde				
Campbeltown	6			
Dumbarton	46			
Dunoon	7			
Greenock	7			
Kilmarnock	37		Strathclyde	
Oban	3		183	736
Paisley	32			
Rothesay	4	142		
South Strathclyde				
Dumfries & Galloway				
Airdrie	77			
Ayr	25			
Hamilton	87			
Lanark	2			
Dumfries	38		Dumfries &	
Kirkcudbright	—		Galloway	
Stranraer	10	239	21	69
Lothian and Borders				
Edinburgh	131			
Duns	2		Lothian 8	
Haddington	10		Borders	
Jedburgh	8		109	304
Linlithgow	36			
Peebles	—			
Selkirk	8	195		
Tayside, Central and Fife				
Dundee	65		Tayside	
Arbroath	41		24	208
Forfar	40			
Perth	38			
Alloa	13		Central	
Stirling	23		2	62
Falkirk	24			
Cupar	14		Fife	
Dunfermline	21			
Kirkcaldy	39	318	10	84

TABLE 2 *contd.*

Grampian, Highlands &
  Islands

Aberdeen	148		Grampian ⎱	
Banff	9		40 ⎰	221
Elgin	22			
Peterhead	—			
Stonehaven	2			
Dingwall	14			
Dornoch	1			
Inverness	41			
Fort William	4			
Lochmaddy	—		Northern	
Portree	—			
Stornoway	7			
Kirkwall	1			
Lerwick	—			
Tain	—			
Wick	16	265	15	99
Total courts		1379		
Total police			404	
Grand total				1783

TABLE 3

*Requests for psychiatric reports in relation to population and to persons
proceeded against for crimes and offences by police area*

Police area	Population in 1000s	Persons proceeded against	Reports	P.P.A. per 1000 of population	Psychiatric reports per 1000 of population	Psychiatric reports per 1000 of p.p.a.
Dumfries & Galloway	143.5	6,847	69	47.7	0.48	10.1
Lothian & Borders	850.8	37,934	304	44.6	0.36	8.0
Grampian	464.2	18,123	221	39.0	0.48	12.2
Strathclyde	2445.3	113,627	736	46.5	0.30	6.5
Tayside	402.9	19,408	208	48.2	0.52	10.7
Fife	343.1	9,913	84	28.9	0.24	8.5
Central	271.8	11,347	62	41.7	0.22	5.5
	5179.4	228,141	1783	44.0	0.34	7.8

TABLE 4

Total reported requests for psychiatric reports in 1979 and sample cases from those totals by area

	POLICE		PROCURATOR FISCAL			SHERIFF CLERK		
	Total	Sample		Total	Sample		Total	Sample
GLASGOW & STRATHKELVIN								
			Glasgow	118	28	Glasgow	110	25
NORTH STRATHCLYDE								
			Campbeltown	5	2	Campbeltown	2	1
			Dumbarton	46	12	Dumbarton	—	—
			Dunoon	1	1	Dunoon	6	2
			Greenock	7	3	Greenock	—	—
STRATHCLYDE	183	44	Kilmarnock	25	4	Kilmarnock	14	—
			Oban	3	1			
			Paisley	32	9	Paisley	—	—
			Rothesay	4	1			
				123	33		22	3
SOUTH STRATHCLYDE, DUMFRIES & GALLOWAY								
			Airdrie	17	5	Airdrie	60	15
			Ayr	22	7	Ayr	8	3
			Hamilton	45	11	Hamilton	50	12
			Lanark	2	—	Lanark	2	1
DUMFRIES & GALLOWAY	21	5	Dumfries	21	6	Dumfries	20	5
			Kirkcudbright					
			Stranraer	10	4	Stranraer	—	—
				117	33		140	36

TABLE 4 *contd.*

LOTHIAN & BORDERS

LOTHIAN & BORDERS	109	30

LOTHIAN & BORDERS					
Edinburgh	67	17	Edinburgh	100	25
Duns	2	1			
Haddington	2	1	Haddington	10	4
Jedburgh	—	—	Jedburgh	8	3
Linlithgow	25	7	Linlithgow	14	4
Peebles	—	—			
Selkirk	8	3	Selkirk	6	2
	104	29		138	38

TAYSIDE, CENTRAL & FIFE

TAYSIDE	24	7
CENTRAL	2	1
FIFE	10	3

TAYSIDE, CENTRAL & FIFE					
Dundee	65	17	Dundee	—	—
Arbroath	9	3	Arbroath	36	10
Forfar	40	11	Forfar	—	—
Perth	29	8	Perth	24	6
Alloa	—	—	Alloa	13	4
Stirling	8	4	Stirling	18	4
Falkirk	16	5	Falkirk	17	5
Cupar	14	3	Cupar	—	—
Dunfermline	—	—	Dunfermline	21	6
Kirkcaldy	14	3	Kirkcaldy	26	7
	195	54		155	42

TABLE 4 *contd.*

Region			Sheriff Court area			Court		
GRAMPIAN	40	11	**GRAMPIAN, HIGHLANDS & ISLANDS**					
			Aberdeen	129	35	Aberdeen	103	25
			Banff	9	2	Banff	—	—
			Elgin	22	—	Elgin	6	—
			Peterhead	—	1	Peterhead	—	—
			Stonehaven	2		Stonehaven	—	—
			Dingwall	8	2	Dingwall	8	3
			Dornoch	1	1	Dornoch	—	—
			Inverness	7	2	Inverness	39	11
			Fort William	2	2	Fort William	3	1
			Lochmaddy	—				
			Portree	—				
			Stornoway	7				
			Kirkwall	1	1	Kirkwall	—	—
			Lerwick	—		Lerwick	—	—
			Tain	—				
NORTHERN	15	4	Wick	16	5	Wick	—	—
				204	51		159	40
404	105			861	228		724	184

Text of Questionnaire used for Sample Cases

MENTAL ABNORMALITY IN ARREST AND PROSECUTION PROCESS

Procurator Fiscal . . . .
Fiscal No. . . . .
Name of case . . . .   DOB . . . .   Marital Status . . . .
The above case is included in the sample of cases we wish to look at in detail and we would be grateful if you could either complete the information or send us photocopies of relevant documents from which we ourselves can abstract it. Should you prefer to send original documents we will return these carefully in due course.

Date of incident: . . . .
Summary of incident: . . . .
. . . .
. . . .
Crime or offence: . . . .
. . . .
. . . .
Previous convictions. (Summarise or attach photocopy): . . . .
. . . .
. . . .
Reason for request for psychiatric report: (e.g. nature of offence, past history etc.):
. . . .
. . . .
. . . .
Time allowed for psychiatric report to be made: . . . . days.
If remanded for psychiatric report, was this to prison, or hospital as an outpatient, or while on bail: . . . .
. . . .
Request made by . . . .   at . . . .   date . . . .
If any documentation accompanied or followed such a request, please attach photocopy.
Examination by Dr.: . . . .   at . . . .   date . . . .
(GP/Police Surgeon/Psychiatrist/Other)
Was the report received sufficiently in advance of further court proceedings? . . . . . .
Doctor's opinion: . . . .
. . . .

PLEASE SEND PHOTOCOPY OF ANY WRITTEN MEDICAL REPORT

Subsequent action/decision/outcome: . . . .
. . . .
If hospital admission, which hospital and under which Section of Mental Health Act 1960 or Criminal Procedure (Scotland) Act 1975 . . . .
. . . .
Did this case cause any problems e.g. delay in access to medical advice/hospital admission/behaviour of person concerned while in custody? Please detail: . . . .
. . . .
Could this incident have been handled by other means had suitable medical resources or service been available? . . . .
. . . .
. . . .

References

CHAPTER 1

1. Discussed in article by F H McClintock in *Le Travail avec les familles de jeunes marginaux* (1980).
2. *See* F H McClintock, 'Some aspects of discretion in criminal justice processes', in M Brusten (ed), *Delinquency Prevention* (1984).
3. *See* A E Bottoms and R H Preston (eds), *The Coming Penal Crisis* (Scottish Academic Press, Edinburgh1980); and M Adler and S Asquith (eds), *Discretion and Welfare* (Scottish Academic Press, Edinburgh 1981), including article by F H McClintock on 'Some Aspects of Discretion in Criminal Justice'.
4. *See* article by Jerome Hall in H H Jescheck and G Kaiser (eds), *Die Verglachung als Methode der Strafrechtswissenschaft und der Kriminologie* (1980), pp 39–52.

CHAPTER 2

1. D Chiswick, 'Insanity in bar of trial: A State Hospital Study', *British Journal of Psychiatry* (1978) **132**, 598–601.
2. Home Office and Department of Health and Social Security, *Report of the Committee on Mentally Abnormal Offenders* (Chairman: Lord Butler), Cmnd 6244 (HMSO, London 1975).
3. Scottish Home and Health Department and Crown Office, *Second Report on Criminal Procedure: Scotland* (Chairman: Lord Thomson), Cmnd 6218 (HMSO, Edinburgh 1975).
4. Department of Health and Social Security, Home Office, Welsh Office, Lord Chancellor's Department, *Reform of Mental Health Legislation,* Cmnd 8405 (HMSO, London 1981).

CHAPTER 3

1. It is worth noting that Gibbens has suggested that laymen tend to overestimate the 'dangerousness' of the mentally disordered offender because his motives often seem unintelligible. *See* T C N Gibbens, K L Soothill and P J Pope, *Medical Remands in the Criminal Courts* (OUP 1977).
2. John Alderson, *Policing Freedom* (Macdonald and Evans, London 1979).
3. See: *Criminal Statistics (Scotland) 1979: persons proceeded against*. Property cases form 16% of persons proceeded against but only 5% of the sample.
4. Home Office and Department of Health and Social Security, *Report of the Committee on Mentally Abnormal Offenders* (Chairman: Lord Butler), Cmnd 6244 (HMSO, London 1975). Chapter 11 Conclusion No. 5.
5. This point was discussed by Sir John Wood, Professor of Law, University of Sheffield in the Fifty-fifth Maudsley Lecture entitled, 'The impact of legal modes of thought upon the practice of psychiatry' delivered before the Royal College of Psychiatrists, 20 November 1981 and published in *British Journal of Psychiatry* (1982) **140**, 551–7.
6. Scottish Health Services Council 1968 (Harper Committee), *Forensic Psychiatry*: in Chapter V, para. 65, it was recommended that the police should make increasing use of the expanding local authority services whose personnel 'may be able to arrange care and treatment for the minor offender'; but this has not taken place.

CHAPTER 4

1. *Royal Commission on Criminal Procedure*, January 1981, Cmnd 8092.

2. Detailed proposals are now published: *An Independent Prosecution Service for England and Wales*, Cmnd 9074 (HMSO, October 1983).

3. It is beyond the scope of the current study, but has important implications for law and society and warrants some critical review.

4. See *Keeping Offenders Out of Court: Further Alternatives to Prosecution* (The Stewart Report) Cmnd 8958 (HMSO, July 1983), for suggested extensions to this decision-making role.

5. R W Renton and H H Brown, *Criminal Procedure according to the Law of Scotland,* G H Gordon (ed) 5th edn (W Green & Sons, Edinburgh 1983).

6. See *Criminal Statistics (Scotland) 1979*: murders made known 47, culpable homicide made known 120; from total crimes made known of 346, 680.

7. 'There is room for almost every degree of mental disorder and of tendencies to deliberate criminal acts within the same person' (*Forensic Psychiatry,* Scottish Health Services Council 1968 (Harper Committee).

8. J K Binns, J M Carlisle, D H Nimmo, R H Park, N A Todd, 'Remanded in Hospital for Psychiatric Examination', *British Journal of Psychiatry* (1969) **115**, 1125–32.

9. This relates to Scotland. A much wider and more detailed study in relation to Magistrates' Courts in England is currently being carried out at the Institute of Criminology in Cambridge with Home Office funding.

10. Gibbens *et al., Medical Remands in the Criminal Courts* (OUP 1977), point out that in their research in England it was the case that where remand was to prison, the report was prepared by a prison medical officer, and where a person was on bail, the report was by an outside NHS consultant. This is *not* the case in Scotland where, except for one prison, reports on persons remanded in prison are prepared by outside consultants and usually the procurator fiscal chooses the psychiatrist. This freedom within the Scottish system seems to deal with the point made by Gibbens *et al.* that it is important that 'justice must be administered by the courts and not by doctors and that extreme or eccentric psychiatric views are not allowed to exert undue influence on the courts'.

11. But one report in the sample had the comment that the writer had 'prepared his report solely from information given by the accused', and others might have been prepared in the same way without including the 'disclaimer'.

12. 'Ordained': i.e. liberated from custody to appear in court at a later date and required to undergo psychiatric examination in intervening period.

13. In the report of the Harper Committee in 1968 (*Forensic Psychiatry, op cit.*) it was noted that it was only in special circumstances that remand need be in police or prison custody (para. 72) and so a remand of a fortnight was little hardship. It was also noted that psychiatrists then felt they could make better assessments when an offender was seen on an out-patient basis (para. 74).

14. During the research project this dilemma was tragically highlighted when a prisoner remanded from court to a mental hospital walked out unhindered from its grounds and murdered three members of his family. Some of the issues raised in the subsequent inquiry are discussed in Chapter 7.

CHAPTER 5

1. A name check on the register of total cases showed an overlap between procurator fiscal and sheriff clerk of 206 persons.

2. Sheriffs are referred to throughout because most cases are handled in the Sheriff Courts, but cases of murder must, and other serious crimes may, end before a Judge in the High Court.

3. *See* W M Donovan and K P O'Brien, 'Psychiatric Court reports—too many or too few?' *Medicine, Science and the Law* (1981), **31**, 153–8.

4. Only a planned period of participant observation could provide such information.

5. Criminal Justice (Scotland) Act 1975: Sec. 180(4) states '. . . the court shall send a statement of the reasons for which the court is of opinion that an inquiry ought to be made . . . and of any information before the court about his physical or mental condition'.

6. The detoxification centres recommended in the Criminal Justice (Scotland) Act 1980 which should remove the drunk and incapable offender from the lower courts have yet to be provided.

7. N Walker, *Sentencing in a Rational Society,* (Pelican Books 1972), p 127.

8. *See* Gibbens *et al., Medical Remands in the Criminal Courts,* (OUP 1977), pp 35 *et seq.*

9. Scottish Home and Health Department, *Prisons in Scotland,* Cmnd 8421 (1980): this is likely to decrease as a consequence of the Bail (Scotland) Act 1980.

110. N Walker and S McCabe, *Crime and Insanity in England and Wales,* (Edinburgh University Press, 1973), vol II, p 90.

11. *op. cit.* p 261

12. *Criminal Statistics (Scotland) 1979,* Cmnd 8215 (HMSO).

13. This is one of the topics discussed in Chapter 53 of the *Second Report on Criminal Procedure in Scotland* (The Thomson Committee) Scottish Home and Health Department and Crown Office, Cmnd 6218 (1975). *See also* Chiswick, *op. cit.*

14. N Walker and S McCabe, *op. cit.* p 79. The traditional approach of the law to the problem of the disordered offender was to ask a jury the question, 'Could he help what he is charged with?' Instead [the English Mental Health Acts] asked, 'What is the most expedient (or 'suitable') way of dealing with him—psychiatrically or penally?', and they put this question not to the jury but to the sentencer.

CHAPTER 6

1. Royal College of Psychiatrists, *Secure Facilities for Psychiatric Patients: A Comprehensive Policy* (London 1980).

2. J H Orr, 'The imprisonment of mentally disordered offenders', *British Journal of Psychiatry* (1978), **133**, 194–9.

3. *Royal Commission on the Law relating to Mental Illness and Mental Deficiency, 1954–57.* (Chairman: Lord Percy), Cmnd 169 (London, HMSO).

4. Department of Health and Social Security, Home Office, Welsh Office, Lord Chancellor's Department, *Reform of Mental Health Legislation,* Cmnd 8405 (HMSO, London 1981).

5. G Robertson, 'The 1959 Mental Health Act of England and Wales: changes in the use of its criminal provisions', in J Gunn and D P Farrington (eds), vol 1, *Abnormal Offenders, Delinquency and the Criminal Justice System* (Wiley, Chichester 1982).

6. B Wootton, *Crime and Penal Policy—Reflections on Fifty Years' Experience* (George Allen and Unwin, London 1978).

7. S A Mednick and B Hutchings, 'Genetic and psychophysiological factors in asocial behaviour', in R D Hare and D Schalling (eds), *Psychopathic Behaviour: Approaches to Research* (Wiley, Chichester 1978).

8. H Cleckley, *The Mask of Sanity* (4th edn) (C V Mosby & Co, St Louis 1964)

9. M A Plant, *Drinking and Problem Drinking* (Junction Books, London 1982).

10. R E Kendell, 'Alcoholism: a medical or a political problem?', *British Medical Journal* (1979), **1**, 367–71.

11. Department of Health and Social Security, *Drinking Sensibly* (HMSO, London 1981).

12. 'What shall we do with the drunken citizen?' (leading article), *British Medical Journal* (1982), **285**, 323–4.

13. J R Hamilton, A Griffith, B Ritson and R C B Aitken, *Detoxification of habitual drunken offenders* (Scottish Home and Health Department, Edinburgh 1978).

14. Federation of Alcoholic Rehabilitation Establishments, *Dealing with drunkenness: a proposal for change* (Chairman: Lord Donaldson) (London 1982).

15. G Edwards, 'British policies on opiate addiction: ten years' working of the revised response, and options for the future, *British Journal of Psychiatry* (1979), **134**, 1–13.

16. G D Wiepert, P T d'Orban and T H Bewley, 'Delinquency by Opiate addicts treated at two London clinics', *British Journal of Psychiatry* (1979), **134**, 14–23.

17. Scottish Association for the Study of Delinquency and Scottish Association for the Care and Resettlement of Offenders, 'Working Party Report on Persistent Petty Offenders' (1983).

18. H R Rollin, 'The Mental Health Act 1959: with special reference to the mentally abnormal offender', in S Crown (ed), *Practical Psychiatry*, vol. I (Northwood Books, London 1981).

19. R Bluglass, *Psychiatry, the law and the offender—present dilemmas and future prospects.* The Seventh Denis Carroll Memorial Lecture (Institute for the Study and Treatment of Delinquency, London 1980).

CHAPTER 7

1. Hansard, *House of Commons Parliamentary Debates,* Issue No 1190, 18–19 December 1980, Part II (HMSO, London 1980).

2. S Dell, 'Transfer of special hospital patients to the National Health Service', *British Journal of Psychiatry* (1980), **136**, 222–34.

3. P Bowden, 'Men remanded into custody for medical reports: the selection for treatment', *British Journal of Psychiatry* (1980), **133**, 320–31.

4. D Chiswick, 'Section 31 of the Mental Health (Scotland) Act 1960—compulsory crisis intervention?', *International Journal of Law and Psychiatry* (1980), **3**, 435–41.

5. Department of Health and Social Security, Home Office, Welsh Office, Lord Chancellor's Department, *Reform of Mental Health Legislation,* Cmnd 8405 (HMSO, London 1981).

6. J R Hamilton and H Freeman, *Dangerousness: Psychiatric Assessment and Management* (Royal College of Psychiatrists (Gaskell Books), London 1982).

7. D Hill, 'Public attitudes to mentally abnormal offenders', in J Gunn and D P Farrington (eds), *Abnormal Offenders, Delinquency, and the Criminal Justice System,* vol 1 (Wiley, Chichester 1982).

8. R Bluglass, 'Regional secure units and interim security for psychiatric patients', *British Medical Journal* (1978), **1**, 489 93.

CHAPTER 8

1. Quoted in A R Matthews, 'Observation on Police Policy and Procedures for emergency detention of the mentally ill', *Journal of Criminal Law, Criminology and Police Science* (1970), **61**, 283.
2. H R Rollin, *The Mentally Abnormal Offender and the Law* (Pergamon, Oxford 1968), p 121.
3. The Harper Committee, *op. cit.*, commenting on the Mental Health (Scotland) Act 1960, said: '. . . some expectation arose and was disappointed that the problem of the "psychopathic offender" would be removed from the penal services . . . .'
4. *Committee of Inquiry into the United Kingdom Prison Services: The May Report,* Cmnd 7673 (HMSO 1979), 4.26. 'The purpose of the detention of convicted prisoners shall be to keep them in custody which is both secure and yet positive. . . .'
5. A point made strongly by Brenda Hoggett in *Social Work and Law: Mental Health* (Sweet & Maxwell, London 1976).
6. *See* A E Bottoms and R H Preston, *The Coming Penal Crisis* (Scottish Academic Press, Edinburgh 1980).
7. Lloyd L Weinreb, *Denial of Justice: Criminal Process in the United States* (Free Press, New York 1977).
8. UN working paper prepared for the World Congress on the Prevention of Crime held in Geneva in 1975.
9. Report of the Stewart Committee, *Alternatives to Prosecution* (HMSO 1983).
10. *See* M Adler and S Asquith, *Discretion and Welfare* (Heinemann, London 1981), and S R Moody and J Tombs, *Prosecution in the Public Interest* (Scottish Academic Press, Edinburgh 1982), especially Chapter 7.
11. Lloyd L Weinreb, *op. cit.*
12. Joan F S King (ed), *Control Without Custody?* (Cropwood Papers, Institute of Criminology, Cambridge 1976).
13. Jean Floud and Warren Young, *Dangerousness and Criminal Justice* (Heinemann, London 1981); A E Bottoms, 'Reflections and Renaissance of Dangerousness', in *Howard Journal* (1977); and John W Hinton (ed), *Dangerousness: Problems of assessment and prediction* (Allen & Unwin, London 1983); and John R Hamilton and Hugh Freeman (eds), *Dangerousness: Psychiatric Assessment and Management* (Royal College of Psychiatrists (Gaskell Books), London 1982).

Select Bibliography

SOME PUBLICATIONS OF INTEREST

Baird, J A, 'The case of the mentally abnormal offender,' *Journal of the Law Society of Scotland,* May 1980

Binns, J K, Carlisle, J M, Nimmo, D H, Park, R H and Todd, N A, 'Remanded in custody for psychiatric examination,' *British Journal of Psychiatry* (1969), **115**, 1125–32 (1969) **115**, 1135–39 (and unpublished figures for 1976 and 1977)

Bluglass, R, *Psychiatry, the Law and the Offender—present dilemmas and future prospects.* The Seventh Denis Carroll Memorial Lecture (ISTD, Croydon 1980)

Chiswick, D, *Patterns of Use and Attitudes towards Mental Health (Scotland) Act 1960.* M Phil thesis, University of Edinburgh, 1978

———'Insanity in Bar of Trial in Scotland: a State Hospital Study,' *British Journal of Psychiatry* (1978), **132**, 598–601.

Elliott, W A, Timbury, G C and Walker, M M, 'Compulsory Admission to Hospital: an operational review of the Mental Health (Scotland) Act 1960', *British Journal of Psychiatry* (1979), **135**, 104–14

Elliott, W A, 'Court referrals to psychiatrists in the Eastern Region of Scotland'. Unpublished

Floud, J, and Young, W, *Dangerousness and Criminal Justice* (Heinemann, London 1981)

Gibbens, T C N, Soothill, K L and Pope, P J, *Medical Remands in the Criminal Courts* (OUP, 1977)

Gunn, J, Robertson, G, Dell, S and Way, G, *Psychiatric Aspects of Imprisonment* (Academic Press, London 1978)

Hoggett, B, *Social Work and Law: Mental Health* (Sweet & Maxwell, London 1976)

Home Office and Department of Health and Social Security, *Report of the Committee on Mentally Abnormal Offenders: The Butler Report* Cmnd 6244, HMSO, (1975)

HMSO, *Committee of Inquiry into the United Kingdom Prison Services: The May Report,* Cmnd 7673 (1979)

HMSO, *Keeping Offenders Out of Court: Further Alternatives to Prosecution* (Stewart Committee), Cmnd 8958 (1983)

HMSO, *An Independent Prosecution Service for England and Wales,* Cmnd 9074 (1983)

Law Reform Commission of Canada, *Report on Mental Disorder in the Criminal Process* (1976)

Prins, H, *Offenders: Deviants or Patients?* (Tavistock Publications Ltd, London 1980)

Royal College of Psychiatrists, *Secure Facilities for Psychiatric Patients: A Comprehensive Policy* (London 1983)

Scottish Home Department, *State Hospital, Carstairs: Report of Public Local Inquiry into the circumstances surrounding the escape of two patients on 30 November 1976 and into security and other arrangements at the hospital* (HMSO, Edinburgh 1977)

Symonds, R L, 'Publicly Disturbed Individuals,' *Medicine, Science and Law* (1977), **17**, (2), 127–30.

Walker, N, *Treatment and Justice in Penology and Psychiatry,* The Sandoz Lecture 1976 (Edinburgh University Press)

Walker, N and McCabe, S, *Crime and Insanity in England,* vol I (1966), vol II (1973) (Edinburgh University Press)

Woodside, M, 'Psychiatric referrals from Edinburgh courts.' *British Journal of Criminology* (1976), **16** (1), 20–37.

Woodside, M, Harrow, A, Basson, J V and Affleck, J W, 'Experiment in managing sociopathic behaviour disorders.' *British Medical Journal* (1976), **2,** 1056–59.

Index

admission to mental hospitals
  from police custody 11
  by court order 12, 14, 36, 96
  compulsory 12, 13, 14, 64, 68, 70, 90
  emergency 21, 25, 81–2, 94–5
  for alcoholism 73–5, 77
  for drug dependence 77
Alcoholic Rehabilitation Establishments, Federation of 76
alcoholism
  in sentencing 53–4, 76, 89
  medical view of 73–5
  social theory of 74, 76
  in sample 77
Alderson, John 19

behaviour
  bizarre, etc. 9
  police action taken 10–11, 23, 24–5, 81–4
  violence in hospital 66–7
  anti-social 70–1, 72–3
  see also police identifying; dangerousness
Black, Donald 2, 3
Bluglass, R 80, 92
Broadmoor Hospital 16, 87
Butler Report, the 7, 12, 26, 39, 69, 78, 80
  forensic psychiatric service planned 92–3

Cleckley, Harvey 73
community care 65–6, 79
  drying-out centres 76
  diversion of offenders into 93
control, social 2, 5, 99
control systems
  medical 1, 3, 4, 6
  criminal justice 1, 3, 4, 6, 93, 95, 99
  communication between agencies 98
  changes in 100
courts, *see* sheriff
criminal justice system
  communications between services 25–6

'gatekeepers' 28, 99, 100
  conflicting aims 89–90, 99, 100
  random working of discretion 93, 100
  special defects indicated by research 96
  ignorance of psychiatric developments 97, 98, 99, 100
  see also overlapping
Criminal Procedure (Insanity) Act 1964 12
Criminal Procedure (Scotland) Act 1975 11, 14, 15, 16, 33, 38, 102–5
criminal statistics, mentally disordered offenders 64
criminality related to alcohol and drugs 53, 67, 73–5, 78, 101
criminality related to mental disorder 3–4, 64, 94, 97, 101
crisis intervention centres
  need of 81, 96

Dangerous Drugs Act 1967 77
dangerousness 16, 39–40, 45, 72, 91, 95, 101
  assessment 92
definitions, medico-legal 6–8
detention
  in hospital 11
  see also security
  in police cell 11, 17, 82
  preventive, a form of 92
Dell, S 87
detoxification centre 76, 97
diagnosis, psychiatric 4, 8–9, 70–1, 73, 88, 95
  in sample 47
diminished responsibility
  plea of 13, 35
discretion
  exercise of 4, 5, 93, 99
  by police 19, 27, 28, 31, 32, 33, 50, 83–4, 100
  in sentencing 89
  see also procurator fiscal
disposal
  mandatory hospital 12, 13, 14, 16, 46, 70, 91

129